Gift of S.C.
Christmas 1971 –
W9-AEI-932

SOMETHING FOR GOD

SOMETHING FOR GOD

THE LIFE OF MARYKNOLL'S BROTHER GONZAGA

+

by
Francis X. Lyons, M.M.

P. J. KENEDY & SONS, NEW YORK

B

C

WITH ECCLESIASTICAL APPROVAL

Second Printing

Printed in the United States of America by H. Wolff, New York

Library of Congress catalog card number: 60-12057

To my mother

FOREWORD

Some Thoughts on a Brother's Vocation

BY ROBERT E. SHERIDAN, M.M.

It is difficult to single out any individual Brother and say that he represents the average. Each candidate brings his own personality and special qualifications with him when he enters religious life. Charles Chilutti, however, held the one ideal that is characteristic of all Brothers: to do something for God.

What kind of a life, spent in the service of mankind in general, represents high-level nobility? It is one in which the zealous, the dauntless, and the brave (and even by the not-so-brave), aided by God's special graces, have an opportunity to sacrifice, to suffer, even to die, so that God may be honored and the bodily and spiritual wants of the needy of the earth may be served.

Who can inspire this viewpoint? Above all, Christ.

And under Christ, St. Paul who crossed over from Asia into Europe to preach the Gospel; Saint Francis Xavier who crossed from Europe into Asia to proclaim Christ to a continent of millions of souls. One follows tens of thousands of unnamed priests, Brothers and Sisters, dedicated laymen in mission lands. One follows every soul driven by apostolic fire, prepared to give itself unselfishly to the service of humanity, prepared to follow the Master in His words: "The Son of Man has come not to be ministered unto but to minister."

The missionary vocation is an appeal to measureless giving, to ministering to the underprivileged, the feeble, the lepers, the outcasts. What phase of the modern apostolate presents greater hazards in a confident sacrificing of self than that of the missionary Brother whose vocation constitutes a holocaust unlimited and unalloyed, of his life to others? To the Brother in a special sense Christ seems to have been speaking when He said, "If any man wishes to be first, he shall make himself last and the servant of all."

To the Brothers at their Maryknoll Novitiate in Brookline, Massachusetts, Cardinal Cushing epitomized the beauty of their vocation in declaring that it was "to give, to give, to give." There is no recompense apart from the consolation and strength that come from doing what Christ counsels, pouring out the coin of life to purchase good for others. How much wisdom in the viewpoint: "Living means giving!"

The Holy Father is, as we know, the "servant of the servants of Christ," and bishops frequently sign themselves "your servant in Christ." The priest is constantly reminded that he is ordained for the people. The Cure d'Ars, model of the clergy, reminded the priest that he was ordained not for himself—he does not absolve himself nor does he administer the sacraments to himself. The hallmark of the servant of God's people is the service he renders.

The goal of the missionary Brother was clearly enunciated by Bishop James E. Walsh, second Superior General of Maryknoll, when he said: "Your vocation is not for yourself alone. God calls people into the religious life to work for others. Your vocation is for the people. When you become totally unselfish, when you think never of yourself and always of others, you will have come to a full understanding of your vocation . . . It is God's path to Heaven for you, and God's Will is revealed to you in every detail of that unfolding vocation . . . May you grow in understanding of the sublime privilege by which you have been chosen to work for others as a member of Maryknoll."

It is only when the Brother, or any other person, loses contact with this spirit of faith and with the sacrificial character of the religious vocation that there is danger of misinterpreting the dignity and the nobility of the vocation. A Brother's vocation especially carries with it the sanctified humble, hidden service that cannot be separated from the sanctity of chosen souls from St. Joseph in Nazareth down to the newly canonized Franciscan Brother, St. Charles de Sezze, honored by Pope John on April 12, 1959, in his first canonization ceremony as Pontiff.

This, then, is the essential of the Brother's vocation—

that he follow Christ in this great opportunity to be of service to others. It is the inspired sentiment of St. Paul: "I made myself the servant of all." Fraternal charity is the test of his sincerity in rendering his obligations to the Master. Service of, and for, others is one of those activities that we can hardly exaggerate. "Love your enemies, do good to those who hate you, bless those who curse you," is the watchword of those who know that they serve Christ by being the servant of His creatures. It is the lesson of the lives of the Saints.

Bishop James Anthony Walsh, Co-Founder of Maryknoll, insisted for all Maryknoll missioners, "Keep in mind that you always seek to serve." He asked continually, "Do you see openings for service and take advantage of them?" He warned constantly, "Many for whom you will do much will fail to express appreciation. Some will later oppose you. Don't let this consideration deter you from doing what you can for others."

The basic motivation underlying every vocation—and most particularly the Maryknoll Brother's—is to serve. Doña Rosario, directress of the National School of Social Service in Peru, made it a practice to give to each of her graduates a wooden plaque on which were inscribed the words of Christ, "The Son of Man came not to be ministered unto but to minister."

This sums up, too, the essential character of Brother Gonzaga, who lost his life in missionary service in the Bolivian jungle. As this life reveals, service to others was his special characteristic. It is a measure of thought and conduct for all others who aspire to be successful missionary Brothers. Their vocation must reach a level that it approximates a synthesis of Christ's two commands: "Have compassion on the multitude," and, "Preach the gospel to every creature."

But service limited to the concept of servitude is still not enough. The Brother's vocation requires that wherever he can, he be a leader and a trainer of leaders. On this subject, Maryknoll's Father John J. Considine says, "The complete image of the missionary Brother reveals him with multiple calls to *leadership:*

"1. Much of the leadership in the *direct apostolate* should be in the hands of the Brothers, from the winning of souls, to their instruction, and formation. The task of *education* of young men calls for many Brothers.

"2. Many activities in the *religio-social apostolate,* works of medicine, of charity, of mercy, should be in the hands of the Brothers. Much of this field, it is true, belongs to the Sisters, but important projects require trained and zealous Brothers.

"3. The *socio-economic apostolate* concerns itself with our fellow man's material betterment, the study and elimination of poverty—problems which Pius XII emphasized so much, and which all thinking people recognize as a powerful answer to world communism. Christianity, to win back its lost millions, must do much more to solve the problem of world poverty. We must stand shoulder to shoulder with factory and farm workers in mission lands; we must use credit unions, co-ops, and community small industries to answer the cry of the "have-nots" of the earth. Many of these programs can well be directed by trained Brothers.

"4. The whole field of *mass communications* in mission work (radio, press, television, and motion pictures) might well be under the leadership of capable Brothers.

"Why is a priest engaged in such activities? Through default of Brothers to carry the load. The priest is the pastor of souls, the catalyst and instigator of everything of good for the people. But his domain of labor is the spiritual. Other related activities should be in the hands of professional career men, who should, by preference, be Brothers. The layman may be able to give three to five years of his life to full-time mission service, but the ideal long-term career man is the Brother.

"We face gigantic questions in today's apostolate and should use every source God makes available. The vast reservoir of spiritual dedication, of intellect, of courage, of capacity for leadership found in our admirable young men who are ready to enter our religious Brotherhoods should be harnessed for the world apostolate. We must open the vision before them."

Thus the Maryknoll Brother must do even more than serve. He must dedicate his ministry to stirring those whose language, customs, racial background he does not yet know. By his example he demonstrates that the apostle must choose a stranger to be the object of his labors. He must consider nothing beneath his dignity, nothing too low for his sacrificial consecration to others. The Missionary Brother yearns to prompt his fellow Christians even by thousands to make their lives the reflection of Christ washing the feet of His apostles. His unselfish zeal leads him to prompt others to bring Christ's message to the poorest of God's poor. No career in the world demands more courage, more persevering conviction, greater spiritual motivation.

SOMETHING FOR GOD

CHAPTER 1

A hush fell over the crowded banquet room as Cardinal Dougherty entered and took his place on the dais, and then the clapping began as it did each year on his appearance for St. John's Orphanage Benefit. As the clapping died down, the M.C. came out on a makeshift stage, formally greeted His Eminence, and then went into a long and carefully prepared talk.

In a darkened corridor off the banquet room a nine-year-old boy sat forlornly, silently fingering a battered clarinet. Both boy and clarinet belonged to the orphanage, but the boy, under the loving care of the St. Joseph nuns, had fared much better than his clarinet. He was slight and dark, and his mop of jet-black hair was still untrained. But there was a healthy glow to his dark skin, and his mobile mouth and brown eyes were alive and expressive.

Sitting there on the floor with his back to the wall, he could hear the drone of the speaker's voice, the occasional applause. But his thoughts were elsewhere, and he kept thinking that it was really unfair to make him play a clarinet when he played the harmonica much better . . . or even the trumpet. . . . Hadn't he played the trumpet at the orphanage to the delight of everyone? And anyway, why wasn't his brother Ernie here? Just because Ernie wasn't taking part in the benefit performance, was no reason for keeping him back at the orphanage. It didn't seem fair, he thought. Why couldn't the other kids come and just sit somewhere in the audience?

Opening his eyes, he saw the Sister standing there watching him. He scrambled to his feet and stood respectfully, just as he had been taught.

"Charlie," the nun said, "don't look like that. You should be happy. You should be proud of the chance to play the clarinet for the Cardinal."

He thought, looking at her drawn face, that she wasn't happy either. And he was right. The Sister was tired and nervous, what with all the responsibility of preparing the program in honor of the Cardinal's appearance; her back was aching, too.

So he just nodded and said nothing.

"Do you remember the night at the Metropolitan Opera House when you played in *Robin Hood?*" she asked, thinking to take his mind off the coming clarinet solo. "And the time you sang the Irish songs for the people at the orphanage? And the other time when you played 'Mighty Lak' a Rose' on the trumpet?"

Of course he remembered, but that was over now. "Why couldn't Ernie be here?" he asked her, knowing why all the time.

The Sister knew he didn't expect an answer. They had been through all that before. Charlie would not try to understand the impossibility of bringing all the children to the banquet hall. Ernie had been one chosen to baby sit with the youngsters at the orphanage. So instead of repeating her reasoning again, she reached down into the deep pocket of her habit and brought up an apple.

"Here," she said, "eat this." And then as an afterthought, "And if you disgrace us out there tonight, I'll give you 'you-know-what.' "

He ate the apple slowly, listening to one of the kids singing on the stage. Then suddenly the Sister was back again, yanking him to his feet and dragging him toward the entrance to the banquet room. In a panic of stage fright, he shoved the apple core into the horn of his clarinet. Thoughtlessly, and perhaps subconsciously in his nervousness, he kept poking it deeper and deeper.

And then he heard the M.C. telling the people about him. Suddenly he was alone out there with all the noise, the smoke and the clapping. He took a deep breath and let go on the clarinet. But the clear sweet tones weren't there . . . just a sour blurp. The silence deepened. Then he remembered the apple core and dug for it. But it was soft and squashy, and it stayed there, way down where his fingers couldn't reach it.

The silence was worse now, and he thought he would die or just burn up from shame. Someone out there giggled. It made him mad, but at the same time it calmed him down. He placed the clarinet very slowly and carefully on the floor and took his harmonica out of his pocket. Then he forgot the Cardinal, the clarinet and the people as he stood there playing an old Italian tune—one that had come over from his mother's country. He played slowly and softly at first and then louder, just a little kid in too-tight-fitting breeches, his hair down over his forehead, his eyes soft and dreamy. Yet all his innocence and sweetness came through and went right into the people's hearts.

They didn't clap when he finished. Quiet and motionless they sat until he began his encore. Then there was the soft whoosh of a thousand pent-up breaths being slowly released. When he finished his second number, they brought the house down.

Charlie didn't even feel the yank on his ear as he passed Sister, nor did he hear her nervous scoldings for his failure with the clarinet. He was thinking that Ernie would have been proud of him. Later that night, back at the orphanage, he couldn't sleep. He felt good inside, and yet at the same time he felt just a little bit guilty about the clarinet. He remembered vaguely that Sister had been very cross, and on the streetcar coming back she had thrown him some awfully black looks.

At the end of the dark dormitory, the same Sister had just come in carrying a candle. She had to change the bedclothes and wash up one of the smaller boys who was sick. He could tell from the way she bent over that her back was hurting her again. So he got out of bed and went down to her.

"Sister," he whispered, "you hold the light and I will take care of him. And don't worry, Sister," he added solemnly, "everything will be all right."

With her free hand, the Sister rumpled his hair and squeezed him tightly. "Charlie," she murmured. "Oh, you Charlie Chilutti, you!"

CHAPTER 2

In a warm bus on a cold, rainy night in February, 1931, Charlie Chilutti sat staring at the darkness outside. The rest of the passengers, including his brother Ernie, were dozing restlessly, but Charlie couldn't sleep. Deep down inside, he was afraid about this thing they were doing.

At eighteen you were supposed to be tough and able to take care of yourself. Back in Philadelphia, in his sister Jennie's house, he had never doubted that he could. But this was different. Ernie and he were headed now for Florida with a few dollars in their pockets. They either got jobs or they didn't; they either made it or else. . . . "Or else what?" he asked himself. Maybe they would come crawling back to Philadelphia.

He had been born in Philadelphia, but his parents had taken him to their native Italy when he was still an infant. At the age of three he was brought back to Philadelphia. But here his father had a hard time, and when the 'flu epidemic came along, he had fallen an easy victim. So the three older children went with relatives, while he and Ernie, who was a year older, were sent to St. John's Orphanage. "Well, what else could my mother do?" he thought. Her health was broken, she spoke very little English and she knew very little except how to take care of her family and her children. It must have broken her heart to see the family scattered. But there were lots of visiting days, and he had always felt that he and his mother were very close. Besides the orphanage had been a good one.

The bus was making good time despite the rain and the wind, and they were rolling through South Carolina. Ernie stirred beside him, and looking at him, Charlie thought of all the good times they had had together at the orphanage and later at St. Francis' Vocational School. It was 1928 when he had finished school and started looking for a job. The first one was with Abe Fischman, making soda fountains. Charlie was an apprentice machinist and he liked the work. But the day the headlines broke in '29—"Market Crashes on Wall Street" and "Noted Banker Leaps from Window"—he knew he would be out of a job shortly. After that, he got work mixing and bottling soft drinks. All this time Ernie had been working for Sears Roebuck. They both had been laid off at the same time, and last week Ernie and he had had a conference.

"Listen, Charlie," Ernie had said, "we can't go on like this—living off Jennie. And jobs around here have dried up. I think we ought to head somewhere else while we still have a little money."

So they had decided on Florida, and now they were on the bus and he was still a little uneasy about it. The depression was in full swing and they knew no one in Florida. Maybe the whole idea was crazy.

Maybe the whole world was crazy. Anyway, it seemed

as if the whole world was looking for jobs in Florida. The Chilutti's checked in at the Seminole Hotel in Jacksonville, paying a month's rent in advance. They might have to go lightly on food, but with a room they couldn't be picked up for vagrancy.

In the beginning the two brothers hunted for jobs together; it kept up their courage. But as the days wore on they split up. Their luck was no better separately, however, and at the end of three weeks they were literally down to their last nickel.

They sat looking at each other across the bed in the quiet room. It was hot outside, the room wasn't much cooler, and they were tired and dirty from walking the streets.

"All right," Ernie said, "let's face it. No job, no money, no food, and the rent comes due in two days. Do we go back to Philly or do we start hitching?"

Charlie wiped his forehead slowly and shrugged. He wasn't afraid any more. After all, they had survived three weeks, and they would probably go on surviving. There were no regular jobs, but there were always odd jobs for two strong kids; and the money earned would provide them with food and a place to sleep.

"Let's toss for it," he said, taking the nickel out of his pocket. "Heads, it's California; tails, it's Philly." He flipped the nickel onto the bed. It was California.

They packed their one suitcase the next morning. Charlie was about to close it, when Ernie came over and dropped the hotel soap and towels on top.

"They owe us two days," he grinned. "We're taking it out in trade."

Years later Charlie remembered the trip to the West as a series of towns and freight trains, one after another.

Tallahassee. A man from California named Johnson gave them a ride. "Boys," he told them, "I made this trip myself years ago. Weren't as many cars though, those days, and it was tough getting a ride." He took them into Pensacola, bought them a meal and gave them some money.

"I'll tell you what I'll do," he said to them on leaving. "If you have what it takes to get to California, look me up and I'll see that you find a job."

The brothers made a mental note of his address: the San Pedro Lumber Company, Huntington Beach, California. They also sent their suitcase back to Philadelphia, C.O.D. It was heavy, and the weather was getting hotter.

Mobile. Ernie couldn't see any use for the overcoat he had brought along, so they sold it for five dollars.

New Orleans. They filled up on bananas, saw the sights and grabbed a fast freight out of town.

Westwego. Outside town they thumbed down a Cadillac. The owner was a nice fellow, well-dressed but thoughtless. He bought himself a good meal and a cigar on the ferry, and blew the smoke in their faces. He dropped the boys off at the gate of a palatial estate near Thibodaux. "This is it, boys," he said, "home, sweet home . . . Thibodaux is up ahead. Good luck."

Just then a Chinese came out of the gate in an old Dodge full of laundry. He took them into town.

Thibodaux. A big heavy-set fellow in cowboy boots and a sombrero was standing on the corner when the old Dodge rattled up. The Chilutti's went up to him, breasting a heavy wind.

"Mister," Charlie said, "we're heading for California and we need a place to overnite." He added wistfully, "We could also use a good meal."

The man in the sombrero bought them a meal and, while they eyed him apprehensively, led them over to the jail. "I'm sheriff of this town, boys," he told them, "and I've got a brand new jail here that's never been used, never even been slept in. It's yours for the night."

In the morning he bought them breakfast, packed them a lunch and gave each of them fifty cents.

Up to this point they had been pushing their luck pretty hard. Now it was beginning to give out. Their clothes were in bad shape from the rough treatment; their shirts were grimy from the dirt of the road and from being slept in; and the gravel of the roadbeds had cut their shoes right through to the feet. Intervals between meals had been getting longer and longer. They were leaner and tanner, but they tired quicker, so they decided to take out some time and get themselves back in shape.

In the Y.M.C.A. in San Antonio both boys washed up. Spying new electric blowers they washed their shirts and proceeded to dry them on the machines. Discovered, they were ejected bodily, the still wet shirts sticking to their backs, the water inside their trousers dripping down their legs.

They were still drying their shirts in the Alamo. when an old man who didn't look prosperous but didn't look seedy either, came up and interrupted the desultory conversation of the two brothers.

"Fellows," he said, "I've been listening to you talk, and if that ain't a Philadelphia accent, I'll eat my hat."

Charlie felt a wave of nostalgia sweep over him at the mention of his home town. He had been writing his mother off and on, but hadn't had a letter in return. Small wonder, the way they were moving around!

"Mister," he said, "pull up a bench and get acquainted."

It turned out that the old codger was living on a pension and odd jobs and making out fairly well. He gave them five dollars. With this money they bought themselves a good meal, wolfing it down at first. Then eating more slowly, they relished the strange feeling of having a full belly. When they felt up to it, they bought rubber soles and heels in a dime store and struck a bargain with a friendly shoemaker. While he mended their shoes they washed his windows in their bare feet.

With a good meal inside them, good shoes and clean shirts, they were back in shape and ready to hit the road again.

In 1931 the roads and freight trains were full of "Hoover tourists," as they called themselves: old fellows who had lost everything and had taken to the road, lacking the extreme desperation to kill themselves or the courage to dig in again; kids just out of high school, jobless and resentful; young men like Charlie and Ernie, who had lost their first jobs and hated grubbing off relatives. Whole families were on the move; there were even young girls dressed in men's clothes, traveling alone or in gangs.

For the most part people were kind. A farmer traveling between towns would give them a ride; policemen in the freight yards let them build fires on the outskirts and sometimes even gave them a helping hand onto the freights, thankful to have secure jobs of their own.

Even so, the Chilutti's ran into what might have been real trouble out around Yuma. They had teamed up with a kid named Bobby Franks and another fellow named Hugo, who had a brother in the newspaper business in New York. Taking Bobby's advice (since this was the fourth time he had made the trip), they gave up the freights and stole a ride on a passenger train. As they rolled into Colton, California, they saw a posse waiting up ahead. When the train stopped, they made a break for it, but the police nabbed them.

The cop that took them in put it very succinctly. "That was a mail train, boys," he told them. "That will get you five years at the least."

But their luck was back. After an hour or so the sheriff came in and told them he had fixed things up. "On your way, boys," he threatened, "but this time, hit the highway. Lay off the freights."

"Sure, sure," they told him. But hardened by now, they hopped the first freight to Los Angeles. Coming into Pasadena, Bobby, the veteran freight rider, told them, "In Los Angeles the cops meet every train. They want to know who and what you are, and where you're going. So we beat them to it and jump off here."

The engineer, who was an old hand at this dodge, had started to pick up speed. But they hung from the freight car door, running crazily and still hanging on until they had approximated the speed of the train. Then they let go and rolled for it, hitting the embankment with relaxed shoulders.

Okay. So they were filthy from hitting the ground, they were unshaven, and they looked like a bunch of tramps. But they were in California at last. The sun was shining; the flowers and the nicely stuccoed houses looked wonderful; and Bobby Franks had an uncle, who was a lawyer in Glendale. They had it made! Just to prove that everything was all right, the first car they thumbed gave them a ride into Los Angeles. Without any trouble they found Father John's Mission—a hostel for travelers down on their luck.

There wasn't any reason for the police car to pick them up. They had cleaned up and shaved at the mission and they looked pretty good. But the cops had a practiced eye and could spot four vagrants at a mile.

" 'Right, boys," said the cop, "hop in."

So in they hopped and were taken to the station house and booked. Bobby finally got permission to call his uncle, but it took a while for the lawyer to arrive. Meanwhile, the four boys came up for a hearing before a judge who had a sense of humor. He asked the usual questions and, finding that Bobby had a relative who would take care of them, he was inclined to be lenient.

"How much money do you have, boys?" he asked. And when they told him they had about a dollar and half among the four of them, he laughed out loud. "All right," he said, "go home with your uncle. But he doesn't know what he's in for!"

CHAPTER 3

Bobby Frank was a big fellow who snored even louder than Ernie. In the end, the constant noise from Bobby's end of the room woke Charlie up.

He lay there listening for a while, debating whether or not to slam Bobby with a pillow, and then decided against it. It hadn't done any good before and probably wouldn't now. So he just forgot about sleep and lay there, looking at the ceiling and thinking.

"The only difference between Philly and Los Angeles," Charlie thought, "is the climate." The depression had hit California just as hard as it had hit the East. It was just as tough to find a job out here as it was there. Maybe Hugo was the smartest of the lot. He had gotten off the freight, stayed one night and then had gone right back East.

The rest of them had spent the first couple of days with Bobby's uncle. He and Ernie slept on the pull-out bed and made so many trips to the icebox that they almost beat it to death. Then Ernie remembered the Mr. Johnson they had met in Florida, and went to see him.

Mr. Johnson had kept his promise to give Ernie a job. Soon they were living in a hotel—three in a room—and working at a restaurant called "The Dinner Pail" for a couple of dollars a week and all they could eat. For the past few days Charlie and Bobby had been running a soft-drink concession on the beach, but it wasn't working out.

"The same old thing all over again," Charlie told himself. "First it was living off Jennie and now I'll be living off Ernie." He wondered what it would be like to go off alone, without Ernie. It had happened once before.

At Alpine, Texas, they had been separated for five days and he had felt kind of lonely, thinking that he would not see his brother again. They had been pulled off a freight in the middle of the night and searched by the police. While the search was going on and the police still had hold of Charlie, the freight pulled out. A bunch of them, including Ernie, managed to scramble back on board. Charlie finally shook loose and almost caught it, running, stumbling and shouting to let Ernie know that he was coming. But then the train had picked up speed and he was alone out there, watching it disappear in the darkness. For a while he had felt panicky and lost. But then he had calmed down and caught the next train. Five days later, he had walked up to a campfire in Yuma, Arizona, to find Ernie with Bobby and Hugo.

Bobby had stopped his snoring now. So Charlie gave up thinking, rolled over and went to sleep. But the next day he had a talk with Bobby. When Ernie came home that night, he found a note telling him that the two of them had taken off for San Francisco.

Bobby never made it. He was knocked out by appendicitis, and when he got better went back to New York. Charlie made his way alone to San Francisco.

It seemed as if the farther you traveled, the worse things got. Charlie picked up a few odd jobs here and there—working mostly for a meal, sleeping in doorways, waking up in the morning with hunger pains. What was worse yet, he felt the cold grip of fear in his entrails. You woke up knowing that today wouldn't be any better than yesterday, and wondering if things ever would get better. You knew that God was up there and that whatever happened was His Divine Will, His way of working things out for you. But when hunger became a knife thrust in your stomach and loneliness and self-pity were up in your throat, you didn't figure it that way.

Charlie was desperate when he shipped out on a freighter for a couple of months to the Hawaiian Islands. For a while he was sick down in the hold of the ship; he thought the ship was going to sink and that he would be trapped. Another time the ship's cook went berserk and came after him with a knife. But it was an improvement over San Fancisco. At least he had a place to sleep and something to eat.

The ship paid off when they docked in San Francisco and Charlie had some money and was feeling pretty good. From now on things would go better for him. It looked as though God had finally decided that Charlie had grown up enough to listen to His voice.

He found a job as orderly in the San Francisco City and County Hospital, taking care of tubercular patients and alcoholics, cleaning the latter up on arrival and restraining them while they "dried out."

The patients loved the little Italian fellow with dark, flashing eyes, tender hands and quick grin. He treated them like human beings—as though he really believed they were temples of the Holy Ghost.

There was a chapel in the hospital and Charlie began to go to daily Mass, serving the Jesuit chaplain, Father Stern, whom he grew to know very well. Father Stern was a stocky German priest with grey hair, blunt features and a heart that took in everyone's troubles. He liked to walk up and down while he talked to you; he gesticulated and his eyes twinkled as he went over your problem.

One day after Mass, Charlie approached the chaplain. "Father," he said, "I've been doing a lot of thinking. It seems to me that God is calling me to some kind of religious life. What do you think?"

"Charlie," Father Stern said, taking him by the arm and beginning to pace up and down, "I have been watching you. I've been watching you at Mass, and I've seen you praying to Our Lady over there, and I know that you have been reading the life of the Little Flower. I'm not surprised to hear you are considering devoting your life to God. But tell me one thing, how long has this idea been on your mind?"

Charlie hesitated about answering. He had never been garrulous, particularly about himself, but now that he had started talking, he decided to open up.

"Well, Father," he began, "I told you once that I shipped out on a freighter. On that trip we put in once at Molokai . . . you know, where the lepers are. Well,

I went on shore and saw all those poor people, some of them with no arms and legs, others with their whole faces destroyed, most of them covered with sores. I heard about Father Damien and how he had given his life for those people, even catching leprosy himself. And then I thought about the way I was throwing my life away, just drifting from here to there.

"I guess in a way that's what brought me here to the hospital—a desire to help the poor and the sick."

He hesitated a minute and then said shyly, "Do you think I'm crazy, Father? I want to do something grand for God."

"I'd be the last man in the world to call a man crazy who wants to serve God," Father Stern told him. "We'll give some thought to this matter and try to decide just what kind of life yours ought to be. No matter how things turn out for you though, do whatever you do with all your heart. And remember, Charlie, if a religious rule is kept, it keeps him who keeps it; but if it is broken, it breaks him who breaks it."

A few days later Father Stern called Charlie into his office. "I've given a lot of thought to your vocation, Charlie, as you asked me," he said. "I believe that you are fitted for a missionary vocation. In fact, I picture you as a Maryknoll Brother."

Charlie was a bit startled, "A Brother?" he asked.

"Yes, Charlie, a Brother. What's the matter, don't you like the idea?"

"Well, nothing is the matter, Father. I just never thought about Brothers. I've been so busy wondering whether God was calling me, that I hadn't really thought of the 'how' of my vocation. That's why I wanted to talk to you in the first place . . . to help me figure it out."

For a moment the priest stood frowning thoughtfully. "It isn't easy to explain the idea of a vocation," he said finally. "God calls you to serve Him and, deep inside, you know it; but the particular form of your vocation depends on you. Some people have a talent for teaching, so their vocation naturally takes that form. Others seek the contemplative life. It strikes me that, through being on your own so long, you have developed a sense of initiative. From what I see of your work around here, you surely have plenty of generosity and a spirit of sacrifice for others. These are the very things that fit you for a missionary vocation. Don't you think so?"

Charlie answered quickly, "Yes, I'm pretty sure I've got a vocation now. If the idea had come to me when I was bumming around or when I was discouraged about my future, I'd kind of doubt it. But I'm settled here now. It's a good job and I like helping these people, so I know that my motive is a good one. But how does the vocation to the brotherhood fit in?"

In reply Father Stern suggested that Charlie talk to Father Cummings at the Maryknoll House in San Francisco. Charlie had been thinking of the missionary priesthood, but Father Cummings suggested the brotherhood and Charlie took this as God's way of telling him what to do. Never one to hesitate, Charlie made his application right away. But before an answer could arrive from Maryknoll, New York, he received word that his mother was ill, and Charlie headed home for Philadelphia. There, on August 5, 1934, he received the following letter:

> Father Cummings has forwarded your application to us, and also advised us that your mother's illness had compelled you to visit home. Now that you are so near, I suggest that you come to Maryknoll whenever you feel free to leave Germantown, and stay with us for a week or two, before any definite step is taken on either side with regard to your formal entrance into our community of Brothers. We always find this best. If for any reason the applicant does not continue here, he does not have the embarrassment of having joined a religious community and withdrawn.
>
> P.S. Maryknoll is near Ossining on the New York Central Line. Let us know when you are coming, but by all means remain with your folks as long as you can be helpful.

Charlie had not liked to say anything to his family about his vocation until he was sure of his acceptance. But it looked pretty certain now, and he showed this letter to his brother Ernie.

Ernie read it and frowned. "Are you really sure you want to do this?" he asked.

"I'm as sure as anyone can be about something like this," Charlie told him.

"Well," Ernie said, "it doesn't surprise me too much. You've changed a lot since we hit the road. You're more serious and religion means a lot to you. I remember all those letters you wrote reminding me to go to the sacraments and all . . . but I don't understand this Brother business. Why don't you become a priest?"

"After speaking with Father Stern and Father Cummings I'm not sure that God wants me to become a priest. It seems I'm better fitted to be a Brother. What you don't understand, Ernie, is that being a Brother is a vocation in itself. You become a Brother because that's the life best suited for you, and because God calls you to it."

"Okay," Ernie said, "it's your life. But the family won't like it."

Ernie was right; the family did not like the whole idea. Charlie went off to begin his postulancy just like a lot of other fellows before and after him. He went off knowing that he was doing what he had to do, but a little disappointed that his family couldn't understand and were not one hundred per cent behind him.

CHAPTER 4

Charlie Chilutti, Maryknoll Postulant Brother, was staring out the window of his room over the boiler plant, looking at the main building of the Venard Apostolic College through the first snowstorm of the year. When he arrived in the fall it was the first time he had ever been in the Pennsylvania mountain country around Scranton. He had liked the way the trees turned color, and now this snowstorm was already covering the winter harshness with its softness and beauty.

The snowstorm would mean a lot more work, for as a postulant, he had a schedule calling for plenty of manual labor. This included seeing that the roads around the property were kept open, as well as the paths leading from the main building to the boiler room, the laundry and the barns. But it was good, invigorating work in the clean, cold air, and he was looking forward to it.

Someone came up behind him and spoke his name. "Charlie," the voice said, "it looks as if we're in for it. When snow starts this way, it usually goes on all night."

He turned around to see Brother Brendan smiling at him. He grinned back, liking this little gnome of a man with his shock of grey hair and his thick salt-and-pepper eyebrows.

"I was just thinking the same thing," Charlie said. "We'll probably have to go on an emergency schedule if we expect the bread and milk trucks to get in tomorrow for the students."

"Don't worry," Brother Brendan told him, "Theophane Venard hasn't let the boys down yet. By the way, did you get started on that book I loaned you . . . the one about his life?"

"No, not yet. Haven't had a chance."

"He was a great one, that Father Theophane," Brother Brendan mused, "went out to Tonkin, Indochina, all the way from his home in France to work as a missioner with the heathen. And what did they do to show their gratitude? They chopped his head off!

"It's a fact, Charlie. They tied his hands to a stake behind his back, and it took the executioner three strokes to do the job. Of course, he was careless on purpose. Just before he picked up the sword he asked the Father how much he would pay for a fast clean job. Know what he said?"

"No," Charlie asked, "what did he say?"

" 'The longer it lasts, the better it will be.' That's what he said! Which reminds me that the longer this snow lasts, the worse it's going to be. Change your clothes, Charlie, my boy, and let's get going on it."

All the while he was changing his clothes, Charlie kept thinking, "The longer it lasts, the better it will be." The longer it lasts . . . as far as he was concerned, the longer he lived for Christ, the better it would be. But you had to live every minute for God or the next thing you knew, the time had slipped by and you had really done nothing. Why, already his postulancy was practically over and soon he would be receiving the black habit of the Brothers and starting his novitiate. Provided, of course, that he were accepted after this trial period was over.

The idea of the postulancy Charlie discovered, was a simple one. As the priest director had explained it, the word postulancy is derived from the Latin *postulare,* meaning to entreat or request. A postulant was a candidate, like Charlie himself, who seeks admission to a religious society. During the time of his postulancy he determines his ability to adapt to the spiritual life and to the self-discipline required. He has an opportunity to seek excellent spiritual advice and to develop the seed of his vocation. The superiors have an opportunity all the while to study the candidate and determine if he has the necessary qualifications.

Charlie had no need to worry about acceptance. His superiors were more than pleased with the way he prayed and worked and got along with the other Brothers. They watched him on the soccer field with the young seminarians, and they watched him on his knees in the little chapel dedicated to Our Lady, where he used to hide out when he had some free time. Finally, they prepared their report for the Superior General of Maryknoll, Bishop James Anthony Walsh: "Reported to the Venard, October 9, 1934. Should enter the Novitiate, September 1, 1935. Has been used as general helper to Brother Brendan. Very pious, good worker, well liked and recommended by the faculty and the Brothers."

Before finishing his postulancy, Charlie learned

about the law of the Church which demanded that, in addition to the postulancy, the candidate spend a year as a novice. In the peace and quiet of the Novitiate the religious society gives the necessary time and atmosphere to develop in the spiritual life and to strengthen his motives and his vocation. It is a serious, spiritual life interlaced with manual training and physical development. Charlie was not surprised when he first saw the daily schedule posted on the Novitiate bulletin board.

6:00	Rising, meditation, Mass, office
7:55	Breakfast, free time, morning duties
9:00	Conference
9:45	Manual labor
11:45	End of manual labor
12:05	Office, particular examination
12:30	Lunch—followed by recreation
1:30	Manual labor
3:30	Outdoor games
4:40	End of games
5:10	Meditation, office
5:45	Conference
6:15	Rosary
6:30	Supper and free time
7:45	Study
9:00	Night prayers
10:00	Lights out

If you were an outsider looking in, the Novitiate would not seem so very different from the postulancy.

You stayed in the same place and did the same kind of work. But to Charlie, there was a tremendous difference. First of all, there was the habit. He wore it all the time now, except when he was in the fields or in the carpentry shop. It felt funny at first rubbing against your legs, and you had to remember to lift it up in front going upstairs, but you got used to it quickly enough.

And then there was the difference in the spiritual life. He had more time for prayer and for reading the lives of the saints. He had already finished the life of Blessed Theophane Venard, and he had practically memorized the autobiography of the Little Flower.

There was also the difference in what you were trying to do. Before, no matter how much you tried to exclude it, you sometimes wondered what kind of an impression you were making on your superiors. But now you just wanted to become a saint, offering everything up to God. You worried only about what He thought of you. You wanted to be humble and chaste and generous, and to love the people you lived with.

Not that you went around with your hands folded all the time. There was plenty of recreation, and you had lots of fun, too.

Today the Venard is a minor seminary for boys of high-school age, preparing for the Maryknoll missionary priesthood. But when Charlie was stationed there, the students were on the college level, studying the arts and sciences for the first two years and philosophy for the last two. They were only a few years younger than Charlie, and he liked being with them.

He spent many an hour with the students on the soccer field and ice skating; and he established with many of them friendships which he renewed and solidified years later in the mission field. He had a way of getting along with people younger than himself as well as with the older Brothers, who made him feel at home. Charlie chuckled every time he thought of how he had been taken in by some of them.

On the feast of St. Michael, who was the protector of the Maryknoll Brothers, a few of the older Brothers had dressed Charlie up in a surplice and handed him a candle. Then they instructed him to bring the saint's relic from the main chapel to the Brothers' quarters. For half an hour he had wandered around asking for the relic, before they finally burst into laughter.

"Brother," they asked him, "where would we get a relic of an archangel? You know yourself that the Archangel Michael never had a human body and, without a body, there can be no relics!"

Charlie enjoyed the joke with them, and he got real pleasure out of being called "Brother." From now on, along with the cassock, he had a right to the title of "Brother Gonzaga."

Of course, there was one more hurdle before he could be sure of his vocation. At the end of his novitiate, Charlie would have to make a formal request to be accepted into the Maryknoll Society, and he would have to take the first oath declaring his loyalty.

But the opinion of his superiors did not change. Brother Gonzaga, as Charlie was now known, was permitted to take his oath, binding himself to remain in the

Society for one year and to dedicate himself to the work of the Society under the orders of his lawful superiors. This oath would be repeated annually for some years before Brother Gonzaga took the final oath for life.

As he walked out of the chapel that day, Brother Gonzaga reflected that it had been a long, hard road, through all the time in the orphanage, the months on the road and in the tramp freighter, the years working in the hospital. . . . "Well, I am settled at last," he said to himself. "I've found my place in life."

But God, they say, writes straight with a crooked finger, which means that He works in mysterious ways for our good. The particular temptations which were now to assail Brother Gonzaga were, on the surface, difficult to understand. Underneath, of course, God had a reason of His own for letting Brother pass through a maddening period of his life. He was not yet so settled in life as he had thought on taking his first oath to Maryknoll.

Brother Gonzaga's first assignment as a Maryknoll Brother was to the Venard—the same place where he had made his postulancy and novitiate. In later years at Maryknoll it would be extraordinary for a Brother to spend these three different phases of his life in the same place. But in Gonzaga's days the Maryknoll Brothers were a young community, experimenting, rejecting and testing aspects of its training program. In 1947 a separate Brother's Novitiate would be established at Akron, Ohio, and in 1951 moved to Brookline, Massachusetts. In 1957 the St. Joseph's Training School for Brothers would be established at the Maryknoll Mother-house in Ossining, N.Y. The emphasis on special training for the Brothers, events would prove, attracted many new applicants. The small group of Brother Gonzaga's time would come to grow to a sizable community of over two hundred dedicated men working at home and on the foreign missions.

As time went on the other Brothers noticed that Brother Gonzaga became more quiet, and Brother Brendan often said, "I got the impression while we were working together that he spoke more to God than to me."

In retrospect, Brother's problem seems simple. He loved Maryknoll, he wanted to be a missioner and, as a matter of fact, he was later to die as both a Maryknoller and a missioner. But suddenly, at the Venard he felt that God was calling him to lead the life of a Trappist.

While he was working with Brother Brendan around the property, the words of his favorite saint kept running through his mind. At the age of fourteen, Saint Therese of Lisieux had started to read a mission magazine, but she found that she had to put it aside. Later she wrote, "Even as it is, I have such a burning desire to go to the missions, that I must not even flick through the illustrations of the apostolate. I would be a missionary, not only for a few years, but I would that I had been one from the birth of the world until the end of all time."

Why, then, did Saint Therese enter Carmel and the contemplative life? Her sister offers the following explanation: "She (Therese) even thought at one time of becoming a nun in the foreign missions; but the hope of being able to save more souls by penance and sacrifice was responsible for her decision to enclose herself in Carmel."

Brother Gonzaga was not bothered by the question of whether or not to be a missioner. He was bothered simply by the form his missionary vocation should take. Would it be better to go to the foreign missions and do the actual labor of conversions or, like the Little Flower, would it be better, by prayer and sacrifice in the contemplative life, to offer himself for all missioners? What did God ask of him?

No one will ever know what Brother Gonzaga suffered during the years that the conflict over his vocation was going on. A lesser man would have resolved the conflict by leaving the religious life altogether; a weaker man would have had a serious breakdown; a spiritual man, like Brother, only prayed all the harder. Wanting to do God's will, wanting to do what was perfect, he hung impaled on the horns of a dilemma for two years.

Long before Brother Gonzaga made his decision, he had the opportunity to speak to Bishop James Edward Walsh, the Superior General of Maryknoll. Bishop Walsh knew men and he knew a missionary vocation when he saw one.

"Brother," he said, "I have been told that you would like to leave Maryknoll and become a contemplative."

Brother Gonzaga stared across the heavy desk at this man who might go down in history as one of the great U.S. missionary figures—at the close-cropped grey hair, the firm lips, the strong nose and the understanding eyes. Brother took courage from what he saw.

"Father General," he said, "I am torn by this thing. I don't know what to do."

"What does Father Walsh, the Rector, say?"

"He has discouraged me."

"And your spiritual director, Father Cawley?"

"He has done the same thing, Father General."

"I, personally, am convinced, Brother, that the Trappists are not in God's plan for you. Your place is with Maryknoll."

Two things developed from this conversation. First of all, Brother was transferred to Maryknoll headquarters in Ossining, New York; secondly, he renewed his temporary oath.

"Here is my petition," he wrote, "to take again the oath of the Society. I am very happy at Maryknoll, thanks to God for His many blessings. Please remember me in prayers that I may be thankful by being faithful."

The certainty that Brother Gonzaga felt when he applied for permission to take the oath lasted less than a year. In January of 1938 he formally asked to enter the Trappists in Gethsemani, Kentucky. He had made a second decision but it was not a clear-cut one. It was a compromise between his desire to lead a cloistered life and his love for Maryknoll. He said later, "I had the idea that I could be a cloistered Maryknoller there."

At 11:45 A.M. on April 8, 1938, he was back at Maryknoll. For a few short months he had changed his name from Brother Gonzaga, Maryknoller, to Brother Mary, Trappist. Just before coming back he signed the following letter as humble Charlie Chilutti:

I can't seem to fit in this part of the Lord's vineyard. In spite of all that has happened to me, I believe it has done me a lot of good. It has been trying. The Reverend Abbot has lent me the money to come back with, and I am leaving Monday, hoping Our Lord will let me do other work for Him and souls. Begging your prayers, I am yours in Jesus and Mary.

Brother Gonzaga was received back at Maryknoll headquarters with open arms and worked there for a while before being transferred to the Maryknoll house in Akron. He did his work perfectly, always happy externally, sacrificing himself for all around him. The housekeeper in Akron said of him, "Brother Gonzaga felt that no job, regardless of its dirty, foul or menial nature, was above his doing. On many occasions, someone would criticize his choice of tasks but his answer was, 'That job has to be done, no matter who does it.' "

And what Brother Gonzaga said was characteristic of all the Maryknoll Brothers. They know that during their lifetime they will be called upon to do a variety of jobs, some of them well fitted to their particular talents, some of them not so well fitted and others distasteful. The important thing to them is that they are dedicating their lives to God, and the particular form that it takes at the moment is not the main criterion. For it can take on many forms, from kitchen work, electrical installations, mechanics and construction on the one hand, to catechetical teaching, piloting a river boat and dispensary work on the other.

Although Brother Gonzaga so perfectly fulfilled these duties of a Maryknoll Brother, he was to know another conflict in regard to his vocation in 1942. He was torn between his two desires: the Trappists and Maryknoll. When he informed Maryknoll of his intention to try the Trappists again, he received the following letter from Bishop James E. Walsh:

> We have your letter concerning your desire to become a Trappist. We were under the impression that this matter had been cleared up once and for all and keenly regret that we have to go into the matter again. Since your temporary oath will expire on September the 29th, you are absolutely free to choose whatever career you wish. However, if you desire to enter the Trappists you must make your application after you leave our house. It will not be necessary for you to remain after the Feast of St. Michael. On the other hand, if this idea to become a Trappist is only a whim, we would like you to state plainly whether or not you formally petition for the Perpetual Oath. . . . In the event that you will leave us again, we want you to understand that it will be impossible for us ever in the future to reconsider your re-entrance into our Society. While we are deeply grateful for your affection and devotion, as manifested while you have been with us, we are keenly disappointed in what we can only consider an unstable judgment in the matter of your vocation.

If this statement seems a bit harsh, it was, nevertheless, just what was needed.

Brother answered:

> The first mistake I made in this matter was when I did not take your advice. I realize that I have been unstable in regards to my vocation. I am very sorry for that and also for any trouble that I have caused. It was a temptation, I guess, brought on by my own stubbornness. God has been very

> indulgent with me and so have you, for which I am very grateful. I am making application for the Perpetual Oath, again asking forgiveness for any trouble I have given and begging your prayers.

After taking his Perpetual Oath, he wrote: "On St. Michael's Feast Day I took my Perpetual Oath. Maryknoll has always been very dear to me, regardless of what was going on within me, and I will try to be thankful by being faithful. Please feel free to do with me as you will."

L'affaire Trappiste was dead. It had been a long, dark night of the soul for the boy who once said, "I want to do something grand for God!"

CHAPTER 5

With his back to the massive fieldstone Seminary building, Bishop Walsh could look out over the heads of the Departure Day visitors, past the Blessed Mother's kiosk in the center of the quadrangle, and on in the distance to the silver shimmer that was the Hudson River.

From the temporary platform where he stood, just a little higher than the dignitaries on his left and the departing missionaries on his right, he could see down into the faces of the crowd . . . the old, lined faces that belonged to the parents of the priests about to leave; at the younger faces of brothers and sisters; on the faces of relatives and friends who had come to Maryknoll on the Hudson, to say "good-by" to the "kids from down the block" with whom they had played and gone to school.

The bishop could feel the hot afternoon sun on his face, and his malaria-racked frame, which had known so many chills, soaked it up gratefully. He turned slightly to his right, running over his coming talk in his mind, exploring the faces of the Maryknollers seated there. For the most part they were the young and eager faces of men just ordained; there were a few who were going out for the second time, their eagerness and newness gone now but wisdom and resoluteness showing through. At the end of the line his gaze fell on Brother Gonzaga who had been assigned to Bolivia.

"Are we doing right," he wondered, "sending out a man who has shown so much uncertainty for so long?"

He watched Brother for a moment, not really seeing him but remembering the letter he had sent almost three years ago. It had been a hard one to write. He had wanted instead to talk to him, softly and reasonably and persuasively, like a father, but then sometimes a father had to use a little severity to bring a son around. He looked at Brother directly then, seeing him clearly for the first time. A slight, black-haired figure, his eyes closed, his lips moving slowly. "He's praying," thought the bishop, noticing the half-concealed rosary in Brother's lap. "At a time like this! Well, Our Lady will certainly take care of him."

Brother Gonzaga was truly praying. The same hot July sun that so comforted the bishop was sucked in by his black cassock and radiated over his whole body, making him miserable and sticky. The perspiration formed on his forehead, saturated his eyebrows and dropped down into his eyes, so that he saw the bishop through a haze. He never had been able to take the heat (his worst time had been the summer he had sweltered in the box cars). He wondered now what it would be like in the Bolivian jungle. He had read in diaries of the missioners already there about the insects and the snakes, but more important, about the intense heat that drained your energy and left you weak and limp.

"What would it be like taking a rusty truck apart in

the hot sun?" he asked himself.

The bishop had begun to talk. "Nobody," he was saying, "needs to ask why they go in this day and age—to do so would mean to be blind to the shocking needs of humanity all over the globe. The people need them, with needs that cry daily to the heavens, with problems that mount to the sky. The people need bread, the people need health, the people need livelihood. They need something to live for and something with which to live; they need sympathy and guidance and help, and above all, they need God."

An elderly woman in the front row of seats began to sob softly, and Brother thought of the housekeeper in Akron who had cried the same way when he had received his assignment. He had come into the kitchen after driving the school bus, and she had handed him the letter. He had gone down on his knees in the kitchen thanking the Blessed Mother for answering his prayers. He had heard that same quiet repressed sob as the housekeeper hurriedly left the room.

"Step out of this country," the bishop continued, "so fortunate, so favored—and see the needs of your brothers. See how the human race lives or tries to live in its material misery and spiritual poverty, and you will understand then why we send them our best gift—your sons and ours, as missioners to be their spiritual fathers. They will build a better world for the people to live in, the world of justice and charity and peace that God intended for them. We have this faith in their mission because they do not build on the sand of human half-measures, but on the rock of Peter."

The bishop was turned sideways, facing them now, speaking directly to each one of them. Brother Gonzaga could feel the words eating into his mind and heart. He forgot the heat and the itching and was beset by an intolerable impatience to give himself completely.

"Fathers and Brothers," the bishop said to them, his frail voice vibrating with affection, "go with God to do the work of God for the people He saved, for the people He cherishes, who are His children and your brothers. Be kind to them, be patient with them, try to help them, try to bear with them. They will not always be easy to help nor will you always have an abundance of means, but try just the same and keep on trying. God wants to help them and He wants to do it through you. He created Maryknoll primarily as a means to help them. He entrusted Maryknoll with the task of reaching them—men, women and children who wait for Him and His salvation all over the world—and Maryknoll now sends you out to fulfill that trust. Go with confident prayer that you will do it perseveringly and well, as missioners of the charity of Christ, as faithful sons of Maryknoll."

Later, kneeling before the bishop and receiving his formal assignment to Bolivia, Brother Gonzaga could still hear the words: "Be kind to them, be patient with them, try to help them . . . and keep on trying. . . ."

He almost missed what the bishop was saying: "To the Pando Vicariate, Bolivia, South America, Brother Gonzaga Chilutti. May God bless you, and our Mother Mary protect you."

Like everyone else assigned to the missions, Brother lost no time heading for the library to study the route that he would have to take and the distance he would have to travel. The section in Bolivia for which he was destined was mostly marked on the map "unexplored territory." But with the aid of a magnifying glass he discovered Riberalta, the headquarters of the Pando Vicariate. He was going to fly most of the way, and he was excited about this since it would be his first time in a plane. He had a notion that he would be sick and, as it turned out later, his premonition was right.

His route took him first from New York to Miami, thence to Cali, Colombia, and from there to Lima, Peru, and on to Arequipa in the same country. Then he would take the train up over the Andes to Puno, on Lake Titicaca, where he would shift to steamer and cross into La Paz, Bolivia. From there it was a short hop by plane to Cochabamba and then another three hours of flight to Riberalta.

A few days later, already on his way to South America, Brother Gonzaga smiled wanly at Father William Moeschler in the seat next to him. He held up his hand, palm outward, the index finger and thumb forming a circle in the familiar sign that everything was O.K. Father Moeschler nodded and smiled back. He was glad to know that Brother was feeling better. Some time before, at take-off, Brother Gonzaga had become pale and had reached for the paper bag that the plane carried as standard equipment. But as the plane leveled off and the pitch of the motors became a steady drone, he had settled back, watching the ocean down below . . . the waves just ripples from the height that they were flying.

Hours later, flying over the Cali Valley in Colombia,

Brother felt a little better. He could see the rich, green valley stretched out down below. But as the plane circled lower and lower, the heat inside the plane increased, and he felt queasy and uncomfortable again. He kept popping his ears and, as he fastened the seat belt, little beads of perspiration formed on his forehead. He could feel the greasiness of his skin as the pores opened up, and when the flaps went down with a "Whoosh," he reached again for the paper bag—just in case.

Then they were down and bumping along the gravel field. Brother was the first one out of the plane and headed for the rest room in a matter of seconds. Father Moeschler waited patiently. When Brother came back, he looked a little pale but a lot better.

He glanced sheepishly at Father Moeschler, "I guess I wasn't made for flying," he said, "or maybe flying is all right, just the landings and take-offs give me trouble."

They had tickets straight through for Lima, Peru. But it was wartime and someone with priority came along and they were bumped off the plane. They took a taxi into the town of Cali and got a room in the Hotel Alferez Real. It was an old-fashioned place with big airy rooms and the mustiness of the tropics. They could look over the main street from their windows and see the palms bordering the quiet back streets. Farther out on the edge of the valley the farms were stretched out in neat little green squares. In the distance the low-lying hills gave contrast to the valley. They showered and took a walk around the town before dinner.

In the quiet dining room they had trouble with the

menu. Brother could spot nothing with which he was familiar. Finally they accepted the translating services of an American who had been watching them from another table.

He was a tall young fellow dressed in a rumpled white suit, and he came over carrying a brief case under his arm. Brother reached out to take the brief case and place it on the empty chair next to him, but the man smiled and pointed to a long chain connecting the brief case to his wrist, where it was fastened with a ring.

"I'm a diplomatic courier," he said, smiling. "I travel, eat, drink and sleep with this thing."

It was the first time Brother Gonzaga had ever heard of a courier and he was full of curiosity.

"Tell me," he said, "what kind of a job is that?"

"Well," said the American, "during wartime we get a little afraid to trust important papers to the diplomatic pouches, so fellows like myself carry them personally between embassies. I came from Miami on the plane before you and tomorrow I'm going on to Lima. From there I travel to Buenos Aires and Rio de Janeiro and then back to Miami. I practically live in airplanes." And then noticing Brother's inquiring glance, he went on. "The chain is to keep me from leaving this thing behind in a plane or a hotel room."

"Well, they must be pretty important papers to get treatment like that," Brother said.

"I never know what's in here," the courier said. "It could be old newspapers for all I know."

After dinner the courier suggested going to a movie. "You'll enjoy the way they conduct a movie down this way," he told them. "We'll be lucky to get out in time for breakfast."

The movie theater was next to the hotel. Although it was after eight and the show was supposed to have started already, people were still standing outside and talking. Inside, little children were running up and down the aisles and no one paid them any attention. Finally, an electric bell shrilled loudly three times and the people began to move slowly into the theater, waving to friends in the audience. It seemed to Brother that everyone in the place knew everyone else. Up in the balcony the *mozos* (young fellows) began to stamp and whistle, and at last the show began.

The main picture was one starring Cantinflas, the famous Mexican comic. He came on screen in baggy trousers and tousled hair and, after the fashion of Mexican movies, talked interminably in each scene. Not understanding the fast-spoken Spanish, Brother sat there realizing for the first time what an awful lot he had to learn before he could become a competent missioner. First of all the language, and then the mentality of these people. But their gaiety and good humor were already finding their way inside him. After all, he was a Latin himself and had a lot in common with the people around him. He felt one worry dissolving! He was going to like these people.

The courier was almost right about the show's lasting until breakfast. After about an hour the lights came on; everyone strolled outside across the street and proceeded to drink coffee and relax. A few young couples with the inevitable younger sister as chaperon strolled around the block. Brother Gonzaga had a cup of thick black coffee with Father Moeschler and the other American as he studied the people. Half an hour later the bell shrilled again, and back they all went, waving gaily to each other once more. After another hour of Cantinflas the whole procedure was repeated. By eleven-thirty the picture showed no signs of coming to an end, so the two Maryknollers excused themselves and went back to the hotel to finish their prayers. In the heat of their rooms they could still hear the sound track booming away across the street and the laughter of the audience long after they had finished praying and gone to bed.

They had to go separately from Cali to Lima for there was room for only one on the plane. Father Moeschler went first and Brother followed him a day later. He was getting accustomed to flying and experienced no more than a passing uneasiness when the plane dropped in the occasional air pockets formed by the Colombian Andes. Flying down the coast of Peru, he was amazed at the barrenness of the land. Underneath was nothing but desert and a thin strip of black macadam road twisting and turning along the contour of the shore, like a long black snake. Off in the distance he could see the formidable Andes. The steward, having finished his duties for a while, seated himself beside Brother and explained a few things to him.

"They call that mountain chain the *sierra,*" he said. "You see the way each peak looks like a tooth in a saw? Well, sierra means 'saw' in Spanish. It looks as if no one lived up there, but in between those peaks are hundreds of valleys where people have been living for centuries. Since long before the Incas, who once ruled this whole territory. Behind that mountain range is nothing but jungle, the Amazon Valley, stretching for thousands of miles, filled with head-shrinking Indians and animals and plants that haven't even been cataloged yet. We've got air maps up front, and whole sections of them are just marked 'unexplored jungle.' If you go down in there, you're finished. We fly over territory just like it farther south and I keep my fingers crossed all the time.

"See that yellow streak of paint on the wings? That's to help rescuers spot the plane in case we do go down. And up in the pilot's cabin we have an emergency trunk full of fish hooks and axes and guns, but I still wouldn't like to try it. You could wander for months in that jungle if some of the Indians didn't shrink your head."

A shudder went down Brother's spine. Maybe you could get to be a martyr in a place like that. Maybe you could give your life for God like Theophane Venard, he thought.

Lima is the "City of Kings and Saints." It is called "City of Kings" because it was on the feast of the Three Kings that the old conqueror, Francisco Pizzaro, came down from the high sierra with a bedraggled bunch of horsemen and men-at-arms and followed along the Rimac River until he finally camped, in sight of the ocean, on the present-day site of Lima; and it is also named "City of Saints" because no less than three declared saints and two Beati have lived here—Saints Francis Solano, Rose of Lima and Turibius, and

Blessed Martin de Porres and John Massias. A remarkable record for a single city.

Brother lost no time when he arrived in Lima in going downtown to visit the Church of Santo Domingo. On the main altar of this beautiful church are preserved relics of Blessed Martin de Porres and Saint Rose of Lima.

Here Brother learned the story of Blessed Martin, a Negro boy who, in the early days of the city, had become a Dominican lay brother. God had blessed him with kindness, and Blessed Martin used to carry all the poor he encountered into the monastery to treat them and feed them. He loved beauty and had gone all around the barren hills of Lima planting trees. In the end God had blessed him still further by giving him the gifts of prophecy and bilocation. Brother Gonzaga walked up the length of the quiet church and prayed silently to Blessed Martin and Saint Rose for help in this new land of theirs.

But Gonzaga's greatest thrill and his greatest feeling of spiritual help came at the little Church of St. Rose several blocks away. It is more a chapel than a church and it sits in one of the oldest parts of the town. Across the street on the corner of the narrow plaza, the old broken-down buses pull in regularly. Most of the time it is quiet there except on the saint's feast day when thousands upon thousands come to visit her shrine and ask her help. When Brother arrived in the early afternoon there were only a few people about. He went in through the chapel door and his first thought was that it was pretty shabby. He wondered why they didn't fix the place up. It certainly needed a new paint job all over, the benches were old and scarred, and the cupola ceiling over the altar had an immense crack in it. The altar itself was a shaky mass of silver that had long since lost its luster, bedecked with cheap paper flowers and with candles, whose melted wax had dripped and then hardened down the sides and base.

For a moment he was appalled at the way the people had let the church fall apart. And then he went out the side door of the chapel and into the garden where Saint Rose had worked and lived and prayed. There was a well there, just as you entered. Long ago someone had thought of throwing coins down there, like a wishing well, and on that day three nuns were bent over looking down into it, giggling to themselves and borrowing *centavos* from each other to toss into the well. In another corner was a little stand where you could buy post cards and things . . . but quietlike with no hawking or pressuring. The garden itself was a mass of tall palms and little paths among the flowers. At the far end Brother was captivated by the cage of canaries all twittering and fluttering and singing in the quiet sunshine. They were called Saint Rose's canaries because at one time she had kept canaries at the same spot.

But to him the most interesting thing of all was the little adobe hut at one corner of the patio. It was a tiny thing, enclosed by glass to protect it against the rain and the visitors. There was only one small low door; no other entrance or exit. In this very hut Saint Rose had used to pray, locking herself up in there—away from the world and alone with her God. Brother momentarily thought of how he had once wanted to lock himself up too, and then he was kneeling before the hut, praying to the saint for the grace to achieve sanctity in the new way of life that he now knew was his.

CHAPTER 6

Brother Gonzaga flew to Arequipa with Father Moeschler, coming in over Mt. Misti, watching the thin column of smoke rising from the crater of the volcano. They stayed in Arequipa a few days, getting used to the altitude as preparation for the trip up into the Andes Mountains.

Brother learned that the trip from Arequipa to Puno, on Lake Titicaca, is made by train and takes about thirteen hours, the train chugging and smoking its way through mountain passes and over barren plateaus as it makes the steep climb from eight thousand to sixteen thousand feet above sea level.

He heard all kinds of stories about the effects of the altitude: how as you went higher and higher, breathing became more and more difficult and the blood thickened until finally you passed out. In all truth some people did get sick, and the train did carry oxygen on board for just such emergencies.

A big, florid, red-faced fellow in the station gave them plenty of advice. "The only way to beat the altitude," he said, "is to keep eating and drinking all the way up. A lot of people will tell you to eat nothing and to drink nothing, but I've made this trip before and I've read up on the effects of the altitude. Alcohol opens up the small blood vessels . . . makes it easier for the blood to go through."

Brother smiled and thanked him for the advice, noting that his friend certainly had a head start in the right direction.

They sat in the huge, leather-upholstered chairs in the parlor car staring out the windows at the occasional stone huts that they passed, and at the small groups of Indians who stood mutely along the right of way. He saw his first llama and was amused at the haughty, high-stepping pace of these beasts of burden.

At noon the train chugged to a halt in front of a small Indian village. Brother stepped gingerly from the train, feeling slightly dizzy and moving with the step of a sleepwalker. The Indian women dressed in their voluminous skirts and high-crowned hats had set up rough wooden tables stacked with plates and dirty caldrons of soup. The Peruvian passengers, immune to the altitude, stood around these tables, wolfing down the hot mixture of lamb, corn and *quinoa*, a grain that grows only in high altitudes.

Brother was intrigued by the utensil they used—a large soup spoon with the tip of the bowl cut off and the remaining edge sharpened so that the instrument could be used as both a spoon and a knife.

He listened to the clipped, guttural language of the Indians, trying to recognize a word or two, but in the end he recognized nothing. His head aching from the exertion and the altitude, he went back inside the train, slumped down in his seat and longed to be finished with the mountains and settled down in his jungle mission.

They came into the station at Puno after nightfall, the little Indian kids clambering aboard while the train was still moving, some of them coming in through the windows, shouting, gesticulating and grabbing pieces of baggage indiscriminately. The conductor tried in vain to stem the tide of grubby urchins, and Brother hung on to his two suitcases, his headache forgotten in the struggle. Finally, he surrendered them to the cleanest boy of the lot and, hanging on to the lad's ragged coat, bumped his way through the train.

They stayed at the Maryknoll Mission in Puno. This mission had been assigned to Maryknollers early in 1943. It already included a minor seminary, a boarding school and several outlying parishes.

This was the first real mission that Brother had seen. He sat up half the night asking questions and listening to the stories the missioners told about the Indians and their work among them.

The older men told him how it was in the beginning. "We came here with a bit of Spanish and no knowledge of the Indian languages," they said, each one adding a sentence here and there. "And this place was in ruins. The courtyards were piled high with rubbish, the fleas were hopping all over the place. We got here at the coldest season of the year and there were no heating facilities. We used to bundle up in all the clothes we had and stand out in the sunshine all day, memorizing Indian words. At night we huddled together in one big room. We'd take the kerosene lamps, put them on the floor and hold the bottom of our cassocks over them to capture the heat.

"Finally, we got the place fixed up. We found some kerosene stoves from the Argentine that would work up here at this altitude. They flared up occasionally and we had to douse them with dirt. They gave you a beautiful headache in a closed room, but they heated the place up and, for the most part, they worked. Except, of course, the time one of them exploded and blew a priest right out through the door and into the patio.

"The people were suspicious of us at the beginning. Couldn't understand why anyone would come voluntarily to a place like this. They thought we were American spies, but we gradually won their confidence."

With a bellow of laughter one of the priests broke in at this point. "Let me tell you, Brother, about an experience I had. I was only up here about two weeks, when Father Arthur Kiernan, the Superior, told me to go out and live with one of the Peruvian priests for a couple of weeks to learn the customs and to get some practice in the language. A priest out in Junguyo, on the border between Peru and Bolivia, was nice enough to take me in for a couple of weeks and off I went. I was out there only a few days when the head of the *guardia civil* or rural police force—a young lieutenant, who was in charge of guarding the frontier—came over and introduced himself. I knew enough Spanish to understand most of what he was saying, but not enough to get out a coherent sentence. The Peruvian priest knew enough English to help me out here and there. When the lieutenant offered to conduct us personally across the border to the famous shrine of Our Lady of Copacabana in Bolivia, I was delighted. The next morning he supplied me with a pass and, mounted on horseback, we covered the nine kilometers in a short time.

"You can imagine my surprise when we were greeted at the Bolivian border by the chief of police of Copacabana. He was graciousness itself and conducted us to the monastery and stayed for lunch. He showed me around the town during the afternoon. That evening, although my pass was good for one day only, he invited me to stay over as long as I wished. We had to refuse since we had a marriage to perform in the parish the next day, and late that night the priest and I rode back alone; the Peruvian lieutenant had already returned to Peru during the afternoon.

"Just before we reached the Peruvian frontier where I had to surrender my pass, I happened to examine the paper with care. It described me not as a priest, but as an American detective. No wonder the chief of police had been so gracious. I handed it over to the sergeant at the frontier without saying a word. The next day in broken Spanish I asked the lieutenant why he had issued the pass describing me as a detective.

" 'Don't try to deceive me, *padrecito,*' he said, 'Everybody knows that you fellows are detectives. With a war on, no country permits healthy, young men like you to go to a country like this, unless they are spies.'

"I tried to reason with him, but he continued to smile knowingly and enigmatically. Tell me, how cynical can you get?"

"But he should have known better," Brother said.

"After all, I presume that he wasn't an Indian. If he was a lieutenant, he must have been fairly well educated."

"He was well educated, believe me," the priest said, "and the Peruvian officers are some of the smartest and best dressed in the world. But for some reason, even though he saw me say Mass, he was still convinced I was a spy for the American government. Of course, no one believes that now, but in the beginning it was a rather widespread idea."

"Then all the people up here aren't Indians, are they?" Charlie asked.

"No, a lot of the people in town are mestizos, a mixture of Spanish and Indian, but the rest are pure Indians who live in small, windowless, mud huts and raise a few potatoes and some sheep. They speak Quechua and Aymara and go on periodic binges. They have a drink called *chicha,* which is made by chewing corn kernels and then spitting them out into a pot. They fill the pot with water, the enzymes go to work, and the result is a fermented drink that packs an awful wallop. On top of that, the Indians chew coca leaves. They take the dried, green leaf and mix it with a little lime that they get from burning the bark of a certain tree. The lime reacts chemically to release cocaine from the leaf. In a closed church the smell is overpowering but you get used to it soon enough."

"How about their religion?" Brother asked. "Do they believe in anything at all?" He knew it was time to go to bed, for he was as tired as he had ever been and was feeling the altitude. But these stories fascinated him.

"Well, they do have a religion of sorts—a mixture of the old Inca beliefs and a veneer of Catholicism that the old Spanish missioners taught them. But it really comes out as a jumble of superstition. Under the old Incas, the Indians had a formalized religion with priests and a hierarchy of gods, the chief among them being the sun god. They even had a form of confession. You'd go to an old man, who was really the guardian of the local shrine, and confess that you had violated one of the rules of the Incas; and he'd divine the gravity of your sin by peering into the entrails of a sheep. Then he'd give out a penance.

"The Spanish suppressed all that, and the religion of the Indians went underground. The Indians accepted Catholicism, but in their homes they still practiced the old rites. Nowadays, they still believe that evil spirits lurk in the mountains and the rivers, and they still placate them with offerings of *chicha* and coca leaves. It's hard to teach them since they can neither read nor write. Few of them understand Spanish."

"Speaking of trying to teach them," another of the Fathers broke in, "I had a very sad experience yesterday. I had just finished Mass and was taking off my vestments when I turned around to see one of the Indians standing in the sacristy. He was an old fellow, dressed in homespun grey trousers, an old poncho and a pair of sandals made out of an old rubber tire and tied to his feet with a piece of string.

" '*Taita,*' he said, which means Padre in his language, 'will you baptize my baby?' I said that I would, and we went to the back of the church. As I picked up the ritual, he took up a tiny bundle from the corner of the church. I asked him the question that we ask of anyone about to be baptized, 'What do you ask of the Church of God?' and stretched out my thumb to give the baby the first blessing on the forehead. I drew away the blanket and saw the baby's face. The baby had been long dead; there was dry blood at its nostrils. I replaced the blanket quickly and told the old man that I could not baptize a dead baby. He told me that he had carried the baby two days and a night, looking for a priest. Then, with that primitive logic that is so hard to answer, he said, 'But, *Taita,* isn't a dead baby baptized better than a dead baby not baptized?'

"For fifteen minutes I tried to explain to him that baptism was only for live babies, and then I tried to teach him the formula of baptism in case it should happen again, but he was unable to memorize the words. Finally he picked up his little bundle and went out into the sunlight with tears in his eyes."

"You're always coming up against heartbreaks in this mission," another missioner cut in. "Last Christmas I was invited out to one of the silver mines back in the mountains. The Englishman who owned it wasn't Catholic, but he kept a fine table, and I had been wanting to meet the people out in that region. I got there the day before Christmas and, as I recall, we had a good dinner. The mine was a going affair, but the little town where the mine workers lived was a disgrace. It was situated at fifteen thousand feet, and the cold was eternal. What with stone huts and the utterly barren land, completely devoid of trees and vegetation, you cannot imagine a more miserable place in the whole world. The Indians were filthy; their clothes were dirty, their hair matted from the grease of the years.

"Christmas morning, with the permission of the mine owner, I set up a portable altar in a dark, unused shed and waited for a congregation. When no one showed up I went out inviting the people to Mass. They sat stolidly and indifferently in front of their cold stone huts, cooking a meager breakfast over fires made of llama dung. I went back to my improvised altar and waited some more. A little boy came in quietly and I gave him the altar bell. We went around the pueblo ringing it, hoping to attract the people. Finally, with only a few clerks present, I was forced to begin the Christmas Mass. You cannot imagine what a disappointment it was. All the time during the thanksgiving, I wondered how long before we could even begin to touch these people and make them understand about Christ."

"There is a lot of consolation, though, in the work," another priest broke in. "Not long ago, Father Kiernan asked me to make a little trip into the backlands to see what was there, and whether we could establish a parish or two.

"I took a train for the first three hours, then got up on the back of a truck for fourteen more. Believe me, it was cold up there at fifteen thousand feet. Once or twice we had to get out and push the truck up a small rise because it had snowed earlier in the night, and the truck had no chains. I rested the next day and then went on by horseback for twelve more hours. Finally, just at nightfall, my horse and I came slipping and sliding down a rocky gorge into a little Indian village. The village wasn't much, even as Indian villages go. Just a cluster of stone huts clinging to the mountainside. Our entrance into the town set the wild Indian dogs howling in the night, and a man came out of the darkness.

"He turned out to be the mayor—a thin pockmarked fellow in dirty riding clothes. He recognized me for a priest, though Heaven knows it had been more than fifty years since a priest had been out that way.

" '*Padrecito*,' he said, 'a friend of mine is dying. Will you see him?'

"We stumbled up the narrow, cobblestone street and into the dark interior of a hut. By the light of a flickering candle, I heard confession and gave Extreme Unction to an Indian stretched out on the floor in the corner. Then, with my eyes burning from the smoke, I came outside and looked around me. It had been a long trip and I was bone-tired. To tell you the truth, fellows, I was more than tired, I was just a little bit depressed and just a little bit discouraged.

"Just then the mayor came out of the hut. 'My friend is dead,' he said.

"I looked up at the stars and suddenly it all made sense again. God had taken me by the hand, so to speak, many, many years ago, had led me through years of study, through eight thousand miles of airways, and recently three hours by train, fourteen hours by truck and twelve hours on horseback . . . just to save the soul of a poor, isolated Indian. I don't want to get sentimental about this thing," he finished, grinning at Gonzaga, "but you can't know what a consolation it was to be sure that God had really used me."

Brother said, "It must be a wonderful feeling to see it as clear-cut as that."

"Don't get the impression," they told him, "that things are real rough. We're making progress, even though it is going to take a long time to make good Catholics out of these poor Indians."

Brother went to bed that night appalled at the immensity of the task that the missioners faced.

The next day Father William Coleman joined them for the trip across Lake Titicaca in the small steamer that, years ago, had been hauled piece by piece over the Andes by muleback.

Brother was interested in all the workings of the steamer, and went down into the engine room and into the chart room, asking questions of the pilot who spoke fluent English. He was familiar with most of what he saw, remembering his own trip out to the Hawaiian Islands before he had worked in the hospital in San Francisco.

They were met in La Paz, the capital of Bolivia, by Father Flaherty, who was bundled against the evening air in a long black cape. They had a problem with the baggage. It was next to impossible to jam it all into the trunk of the battered taxi. At last they had to leave the trunk open and hope for the best.

When it came time to unload at the house, one of Brother's suitcases was missing. They went back over the route, but they never found whether someone had stolen it or whether it had just fallen out as they climbed the steep hills of the city. The loss of the suitcase came as a severe blow to Brother. In it he had most of the technical books on motors, electricity and building that he knew he would need on his mission. But Father Flaherty, who was used to such disasters, just shrugged and laughed.

"Gonzaga, my boy," he said, "you're going to lose a lot more than that before you are finished. You might as well get used to it."

So Brother had his first lesson in staying relaxed in the face of what looked like disaster at the time. Years later, he had developed this virtue to the point where he would look at a broken-down motor hundreds of miles from civilization, and just take it in stride.

Gonzaga was becoming used to the altitude by this time; he could walk without undue fatigue and his breathing came easier. Father Flaherty told him that his body was undergoing a natural process. "You need more red blood corpuscles to take more oxygen out of the air you breathe. So your body goes to work and, in the marrow of your bones, produces more of the corpuscles. At sea level you need only about three or four million, but up here you almost have to double that amount."

Gonzaga spent the next day wandering around the city, studying the people with an intense curiosity. He saw them as a dark-skinned people, neither black nor yet bronze but of an indeterminate brownish color. They were small of stature—usually under five feet—but had an enormous chest development for their size. He noted one Indian, typical of his race, with an aquiline nose, large nostrils, a big mouth with not very fleshy lips and fine strong teeth. The man's square back and large chest caused his trunk to seem out of proportion to his extremities; this gave the appearance of great strength. But as Brother had already learned from watching the porters, the Indians have little power for lifting heavy objects. But once the object has been placed on their backs, they will carry an unbelievable weight for long distances up and down mountains, in a peculiar gait which resembles a dog trot.

At first the brown derbies worn by the women had caused Gonzaga to smile to himself, but after an hour or so of walking around the market place, he had become accustomed to them. He was even more surprised by the brilliant colors of their clothes. The Indian woman wears a blouse of heavy material, usually of a red shade, and anywhere from five to fifteen bulky skirts of brilliant and clashing colors—which she doffs one by one as the day grows warmer. Wearing sandals like her husband, she forms a bundle on her back by tying a blanket's ends across her breast. The resultant catchall contains practically everything mentionable: vegetables, coca leaves, sticks for firewood, clothing, the doffed skirts, small ceramics for sale and usually a smiling, bright-eyed baby. The baby's head is sometimes right side up, sometimes right side down—his position apparently a matter of indifference to himself and his mother.

The Indian man wears shin-long, grey, woven trousers and a gaily colored poncho over a store shirt. He has leather sandals on his feet. His poncho is usually some shade of red, and occasionally he wears a dirty felt hat on top of a knitted one.

"Well, what do you think of the place?" Father Flaherty asked Brother when, late that afternoon, he came in tired and dusty. "How would you like to stay on with us, instead of going down into the hot jungle?"

"It's not for me," Brother said. "Tell me something. Why in the name of Heaven did these people pick a spot like this to live? It is cold and barren, and the altitude kills you; every time you walk you seem to be climbing a mountain. Incidentally, I suppose that the people selling things in the market place aren't from the city. Where do they live anyway?"

Father Flaherty started to laugh. "I've never met a *gringo* yet, Brother," he said, "who didn't ask those two questions. As to your first question, they were just born up here, I suppose; and to most people that's a pretty good reason for living in a place. As to where they actually live, well, most of them have a little plot of ground out on the pampa."

He added, "Sometimes they even puzzle me. Once I left a town with a truckload of Indians. After we had traveled over an almost endless plain for hours, with nothing on either side but snow-capped mountains off in the distance, one of the Indians tapped on the cab of the truck as a signal for the driver to stop. He then gravely descended to the ground, paid his fare, picked up his bundle and started off in the middle of nowhere. Where he was going or how many days it would take him to get there, I have never been able to find out."

Brother made the last lap of his trip in a cargo plane. La Paz and Cochabamba and the highlands were behind him now, and down below the jungle of Bolivia stretched out as far as the eye could see in any direction. The rivers were silver bands, twisting back on themselves, wandering erratically through the green landscape, cutting their way through the undergrowth. The tops of the trees formed a canopy, which made it impossible to see the ground, except rarely when their matted growth was broken by a small clearing.

Occasionally, along the river bank Brother Gonzaga could see a thatched roof or two, but no people. He was excited inside now that he was getting close to his destination, and he kept turning to his companion Father Danehy to ask all sorts of questions. They were the only two passengers on the plane. The rest of the seats had been taken out and the plane piled with cargo. There were bags of rice and sugar, cans of kerosene and assorted boxes of all types. These were covered with tarpaulin and lashed down to keep them from shifting. Over all hung the odor of desiccated hides, which the plane always carried on the return trip; their smell had penetrated forever and irrevocably into every crack in the fuselage. They ran into a storm after an hour or so, and Brother was surprised to find himself getting wet. He looked up and saw the rain pouring in through a crack in the ceiling.

Father Danehy saw his frightened glance and laughed. "It's all right, Brother," he said, "the plane won't sink. Just a little crack, and this won't last long anyway. This airline has perhaps the worst planes and the best pilots in the world. It's amazing the places they put these things down in. I don't believe these fellows have ever landed on or taken off from a concrete field. Just a lot of places cleared out of the jungle. Sometimes, they crack up, but they always walk away from the wreck.

"There is a story about five missioners who landed up north of here. They came in on a slippery, muddy field and just as they touched down, the landing gear buckled. The plane slid the length of the field and ended up in a ditch. No one had so much as a scratch. Another time, the pilot put a plane down in Riberalta and found he had no brakes. He went the length of the field, right through a wire fence and down the street. Seeing that the street ended in a row of houses, he swung the monster around and stopped in the middle of a side street with a foot to spare between the wing tips and the houses on each side. But he hadn't touched any person or even a house! Anyone can fly these things in the air, but these boys drive them on the ground like automobiles."

Brother was impressed, but he still kept glancing apprehensively at the crack in the ceiling until they had passed through the storm.

Later, Father Danehy was cleaning his steamed-up glasses and Brother was wishing he had had the foresight to have a couple of white cassocks made.

"You know, Brother," Father Danehy said, "we're lucky when you come to think of it. Not so many years ago the missioners who came this way had to travel overland. It took them anywhere from three to six months, with a caravan of mules carrying supplies. They used to hole up each night wherever they found themselves. The biggest difficulty they had was keeping the mules and horses from dying. They would come out in the morning and find that vampire bats had been sucking the blood out of the animals all night. It took only a couple of nights like that, and suddenly you had a dead mule on your hands.

"The men used to make the last part of the trip by boat. They had to hire a couple of Indians and some dugout canoes and pole all day. When they hit the rapids or a sunken tree trunk, they frequently turned over and lost all they had carried so far. Often they ended up living off wild plants and fish they could catch in the rivers. Nowadays we settle back in a nice comfortable plane, even if it does leak a little and smell a bit, and in a matter of hours we're there.

"In fact, Brother, that's Riberalta just ahead."

Brother strained to see out the window. But all that was visible was a few houses with thatched roofs, and what looked like two rivers making a junction. And then they were down and the heat was soaking through his black cassock.

There was no band to greet Brother Gonzaga, but all the priests and half of the populace were at the airport. So, half trying to hide his embarrassment he went through a series of *abrazos*—the famous South American custom of throwing the arms around one another and popping the head from one shoulder to the other.

When he came to Bishop Escalante, who was the Vicar Apostolic and Brother's Superior, he knelt in the dry dust, unaware of the effect it had on his black cassock, and kissed the Bishop's ring fervently.

"Bishop," he whispered, "I pray that God will permit me to serve you long and faithfully."

The bishop, a short, bespectacled, happy man, who had spent many years in the Far East, raised him smilingly to his feet.

"Brother," he said, "I can't tell you how much we have prayed for you and how long we have been awaiting your arrival."

CHAPTER 7

Bolivia—to which Brother was assigned—is seventy-eight times the size of Massachusetts and comprises nine departments, each about the size of one of our good-sized states. Two of these departments, the Pando and the Beni, are under the spiritual care of the Maryknoll Fathers. This Bolivian mission has the official title of "Vicariate of the Pando." The capital of the Pando is Cobija. The capital of the Beni is Riberalta.

The town of Riberalta, where the bishop habitually resides, is considerably larger than Cobija. Riberalta has the advantage of being much more strategically located in relation to other centers which can be reached only by the rivers. It is a town of quite recent growth. Seventy years ago, Riberalta was but a clearing with a few houses, and it was only during the rubber boom around the beginning of the century that it acquired relative importance. It is situated on the high bank (Riberalta means "high bank") of the Beni River, not far below the point where that river merges with the waters of the Madre de Dios River. Down river only a few hours distant is Cachuela Esperanza, a lovely little place just above the rapids (Cachuela means "rapid") which complicate all shipping to or from this region. There is a chapel there, and ordinarily a priest is in residence.

A truck road connects Cachuela with Guayaramerim, which is on the Mamoré River. The road is owned and operated by the Suarez interests. Passengers are tolerated on the trucks as long as their presence does not interfere with the transfer of goods. The whole country between the rivers through which the road passes is jungle and pampa, which is the name usually given to the treeless areas on the edge of the jungle. Like Cachuela Esperanza, Guayaramerim is also the residence of a priest. The two towns are about the same size and are connected by a dirt road.

Up the Beni River from Riberalta there are no towns at all, although there is a residence at Fortaleza for the priests whose responsibility it is to contact and care for the people living in scattered groups along the banks of the river and in clearings back from the river. Farther still up river is the residence of a priest who is official caretaker as well as pastor of the Cavina Indians.

Two hundred miles by plane from Riberalta is Cobija, with its fifteen hundred inhabitants, many of them officials. Two priests are normally stationed there, and the Maryknoll Sisters staff a school as well. Nearby is the small town of Porvenir. All this section of the Pando is frontier territory bordering on both Peru and Brazil. Opposite Cobija is the Brazilian town of Brasileia.

The center of the Vicariate is connected with all the main settlements along the principal rivers. Between Riberalta, Cobija and Guayaramerim there is plane service. Other places must be reached by river, except for the connecting roads between Cobija and Porvenir and between Cachuela Esperanza and Guayaramerim. Cavinas, for example, is six or seven days away from Riberalta by river going upstream. But in the flood season the journey downstream can be made in two days, although it will be a very dangerous two-day period.

Throughout the whole of the Vicariate there are perhaps not much more than a thousand pure-blooded Indians—the survivors of many (but probably never very large) tribes, which once fought with one another for possession of this land. The inhabitants of the region are now predominately either of European ancestry or of mixed blood. The European element has drifted into the area from neighboring sections of Peru and Brazil and from other sections of Bolivia.

The residents of the region—whether natives or recent settlers—give hardly a thought to the unusual features which forcibly strike all outside visitors. To the local people, it does not seem at all strange to live in a land where the only highways are vast rivers endlessly making their way to the vaster Amazon and the Atlantic. Visitors, on the other hand, are overawed by the muddy bands that twist and turn through the jungle and the great plains, for all the world like a modern system of superhighways. They can for a moment even mistake these rivers for highways, until they pinch themselves and remember that, in the whole Vicariate of the Pando, there are only some fifty thousand people—hardly enough to call for such a system of roads.

Maryknoll mission work in the Pando began just as the second rubber boom in that region was beginning to taper off. The boom had resulted in some real benefits for the people. One of these was the little hospital built in Riberalta with the cooperation of the United States and given to the Bolivian government. The Maryknoll Sisters, who came to the Pando not long after the arrival of the Maryknoll Fathers, took over the administration of the hospital from the beginning. They have staffed it with trained and very efficient nurses, and at the head of the staff there has always been a Maryknoll Sister-doctor.

When Brother Gonzaga arrived in Riberalta in 1945, this hospital was under the direction of Sister Mary Mercy, who had had previous experience in medical missionary work in Korea—a country to which she later returned.

Once Brother had caught his breath and was able to appreciate the nature of the country, the dimensions of the Vicariate, the difficulty of communications and the kind of work he would be expected to do, he must have felt a little overwhelmed at the thought of keeping so many different projects in working order, especially in an area where it is a heroic task to keep anything—above all, machinery—in shape. The obstacles are infinite in their variety. Nature throws up all kinds of roadblocks, and the human inhabitants are too pitifully few to make any lasting impression on the boundless stretches of a soil, capable of producing so much, but in fact producing very little useful to man.

Then, as well as today, the big sprawling rivers

made their own beds, chewing their unruly way to the ocean, digging new channels as they saw fit, rolling on unhindered, carrying with them the debris of half a continent, at once the indispensable friends and the mortal enemies of mankind. On their banks, and in the spaces between the rivers, the trees grew unchecked, in luxuriant abundance: trees unknown in the rest of the world; trees of species as yet undescribed; magnificent hardwoods used, if at all, as ties for railway tracks and wheels for oxcarts; trees held together by a vast network of lianas, in season flaming into all sorts of exotic flowers and harboring every kind of flamboyant bird life. The fringes of these tropical forests provided shelter for fauna of every species from the dangerous jaguar to the tiniest insects, which represent a much greater danger to man. Animal consumed animal, the bigger preying on the smaller, the smaller devouring the carcasses of the bigger, when they managed to arrive before the buzzards which were perpetually patrolling for carrion. In the rivers themselves lurked mortal dangers: incredible boa constrictors, alligators, electric eels and, most feared of all, a voracious little man-eating fish, the *palemeta.*

A scientist exploring the Amazon area will generally take the attitude that it falls short of all the claims made about it. He will come back proclaiming that its mystery had been overdone, its dangers exaggerated, its attractions overrated. He will assert that it is a very suitable abode for man and could be a very healthy one, too. But the scientist does not make it his abode; he comes back. Those who stay there, those who live close to the jungle, are ever conscious of the jungle. They love it and they hate it, for to them it is both a fairyland and a chamber of horrors. To them the always surprising silence of the jungle by day is almost as sinister as the uncanny noises of the jungle by night. To them the nocturnal whistling, hammering, screeching and hooting reveal the real nature of the jungle more truly than the magnificence of flowers, the fitful flight of the dazzling butterflies, the delicacy of the hummingbirds. The mammoth cockroaches are a better emblem of the jungle than the miniature deer.

It was to this territory that Brother Gonzaga came to begin his missionary career.

In 1942 Bishop James E. Walsh, then the Superior General of Maryknoll, had made a swing through South America to look over future commitments for the Society. In June of that year he described Riberalta thus:

> The little town is lovely, stretching out along the high bank of the broad Rio Beni, well elevated above the swampy lowlands and hence dry and clean. It has a pretty little plaza in front of the church, a fair number of good compounds with comfortable-looking houses, many poor huts, domestic animals in tranquil possession of the roadways that are called streets. It is still very hot here in South America's December (our June) and the humidity is extreme.
>
> Our chapel is a passable and roomy shell of no style. Our rectory is dirty, damp, dismal, unwashed, uncomfortable, unkept, without any neatness or order, ramshackle, ridiculous and wretched. And yet the poor little house is not essentially bad, and generous doses of carpenter's repairs, paint, whitewashing, sweeping, disinfecting and unlimited

> cleaning would make it fairly good. It is a one-story ground-floor bungalow of brick and beam with tile roof, no ceiling, brick floor, good cedar doors and windows, containing three sizeable rooms side by each, plus one long verandalike room running the full length of the house. There are cheap screens on the windows but not on the doors. There is a good garden containing avocado and mango trees, a well with a Rube Goldberg shower-bath contraption and a lot of chickens. There is no kitchen, and the meals are sent in by the family next door.

By the time Brother Gonzaga arrived in 1945, the rectory had already seen a carpenter and had been improved by paint, whitewashing, sweeping, disinfecting and unlimited cleaning. But the town was for the most part unchanged. Brother wandered around the sandy streets, saying hello to everyone he met, giving them his quick grin. In a few days he had met practically all of the townspeople, and in their responsive friendly way they had accepted him into their hearts.

It was several months though before they fully realized that he was not a priest like all the other Maryknollers and stopped calling him "*padrecito.*" In time they came to call him "*hermanito,*" which means "little brother."

Brother spent the first several days checking out his tools, setting up a workshop and studying Spanish. The Spanish language came quickly to him, because of his knowledge of Italian and the fact that he was thrown in so quickly with the mechanics and the children of the town in his work. He was to find out later that he would never know the English for many of the words he had learned in Spanish. Very quickly, like the other Maryknollers, he sprinkled his conversation with Spanish phrases that he never bothered to translate.

After a couple of months in South America a typical conversation between two Maryknollers would go something like this:

"So I took the *camionetta* for a run out to the *campo,* saw the *mayordomo,* looked over the *hacienda,* and picked up the *yeso,*" (meaning, of course, "I took the pickup truck out in the country, spoke to the manager, looked over the ranch and picked up a load of plaster").

The other would ask, "How are the *señora* and the *niños,* and who is *guardandoing* the *yeso* now?" (meaning, "How are the manager's wife and children, and who is standing watch over the plaster now?").

Like everyone else, Brother made mistakes in the language that were laughable. But he was cheered when he listened to the tales that the others told about their own blunders.

Father James Logue, shaking all over with laughter had the best stories. "Brother," he said, "I'll never forget when we arrived in Lima. We were in a hotel, another priest and myself, and our Spanish was negligible. The waiter started to pour the coffee and, since it was pure essence, only a few drops were needed. Thinking to stop the waiter before he put too much in, the other priest kept telling him '*bastante.*' The more he shouted the more the waiter kept pouring 'till finally it spilled over the brim and onto the saucer. It wasn't until later that we found out that *bastante* means 'plenty of it' and *basta* means 'stop.'

"There was another time I heard a priest preaching and he was describing how Mary Magdalen walked around the town. 'There she was,' he said, 'walking around covered with pots and pans'! What he had meant to say, of course, was 'covered with jewels'; but the words are so similar he got them mixed up. . . . That same man kept calling the Holy Father 'the old potato,' instead of 'the former Pope' because he kept using the feminine article instead of the masculine."

"I don't know," Brother said, "but sometimes I feel so darn discouraged. I'm trying to say something and the words just won't come. I know the words and they are inside me, but they just won't come out."

"It's just a matter of practice," Father Logue told him. "It takes time. And it's a good thing too, that we can't speak the language fluently when we first arrive. I remember reading something that a Protestant missionary in Japan once wrote. He said that while a man is learning the language he has a chance at the same time to learn the customs and the way of thinking of the people. By the time he can speak, he knows how to treat the people and their problems. But if he comes out speaking the language from the first day, he is apt to blunder into many situations without knowing the customs. He could cause a lot of harm that way. There is a certain economy in being forced to go slowly."

"Well, I can understand that," Brother said, "so I'll just go plugging along and hope for the best."

He took time out from his Spanish studies and work to write to the Superior General:

. . . arrived safely. Although the trip was very interesting, I am glad to settle down once more. I like the people, especially the children, who are very friendly. It is all very new to me, but I hope it will not be long before I become acclimated. The opportunities are legion. I am grateful to have the chance of helping others out in what God has given to me so freely. The bishop and the padres are real well, and have been swell to me. So far all the places I have been to where there are Maryknoll Padres have seemed like home, for the same spirit has been brought with them, and the people cannot help but be affected by it.

He dropped a note to his sister Jennie about the same time:

. . . arrived here safely. A jungle town, but not as bad as I had imagined. The trip was swell, but I am glad to settle down for a while. The people are poor, simple, living in thatched and adobe houses. Conveniences are few, there are great opportunities for doing good, and after all, that is the one reason why I came, to help others find in life what was so freely given to me, a chance to know God and live a decent life. What people consider necessities in the States would be luxuries around here. I am feeling fine, the bishop and the padres are doing a grand job, and it is a privilege to be associated with them. Hope that Mom and all are O.K. Don't worry, things are swell. God bless you for now, don't forget the prayers. . . .

CHAPTER 8

The first two weeks went quickly in the new surroundings. Brother worked at his Spanish in the mornings and at night. But the afternoons he spent in his makeshift workshop, surrounded by outboard motors in various stages of dismantlement. He was puttering away there one afternoon trying to rewire a small generator, the sweat staining his blue denim shirt and dripping from his heavy eyebrows down onto his work. Suddenly he had the uncomfortable feeling that someone was watching him.

He turned around to see a skinny, little lad in short white pants and a soiled T-shirt standing in the doorway.

"Hi," Brother said, "what's your name?"

The boy grinned shyly, and looking down at the dirt floor said quietly, "I am called Tedzu Yakota."

Brother had been expecting a Spanish name like "Juan," or "José," and he was momentarily startled. But then he realized that his little visitor was a member of the small Japanese colony that had settled as farmers around Riberalta. Gathering his Spanish together he said, "Okay, Tex, grab a broom and start sweeping."

Tex went out and came back in a few minutes, carrying a common substitute for a broom—some small branches from a nearby tree tied with a string. He set about industriously raising a cloud of heavy yellow dust in his efforts to do a good job.

In the meanwhile Brother had formulated several Spanish phrases in his mind. When he thought he had something to work with, he stopped the boy and asked him what he had in his back pocket.

"*Una honda,*" the boy told him, offering the slingshot for inspection. It was made of one of the jungle hardwoods and was as smooth as constant rubbing and oiling could make it. The rubber portion had been made from a strip of old inner tube. Brother flexed it and sighted it out the doorway.

At that moment a shiny head appeared between the two prongs of the slingshot, and an anxious voice said, "Don't shoot. It's a friend."

Brother put the slingshot down and greeted Father Robert Fransen.

"What gives?" the priest asked, "Are you practicing Spanish with Tedzu or is he teaching you to shoot that thing?"

"Both," Brother told him. "My friend Tex here has been teaching me some new words. Now I know that *una honda* is a slingshot, and *tirar* means 'to shoot.' So we go on learning *poco a poco.*"

"Good," said Father Fransen, "and I'll teach you an idiom to go along with that *poco a poco* bit. '*Yendo despacio, se anda lejos,*' which means 'he who walks slowly, goes far.' " Then turning to the boy he said, "Let's have some ammunition, Tex."

Tex dug into his trouser pocket and came up with a handful of small clay marbles.

"I'll bet you, Bro," said Father Fransen, "that you thought they used pebbles with these things."

"Well, yes, I guess I did," Brother said. "That's what I used as a kid. How come they use clay here?"

"Look around you, Gonzaga, and tell me if you see a single pebble anywhere."

Brother looked around reflectively, "Come to think of it," he said, "I haven't seen even a rock since I've been in Riberalta, let alone a pebble."

"That's right," the Padre said, "and you won't see one in the whole Beni district except in the river around the rapids. God forgot to put rocks in this section of the world. That's the reason for the clay ammunition. The kids take the mud, form the balls and bake them in an oven. When you work so hard, you're quick to become an expert. These boys can knock a small bird out of a high tree with one shot."

"Is that true, Tex?" Brother asked the small Japanese boy.

"*Sí, Hermano,*" Tex replied, "and I will teach you to shoot also."

"Good," Brother said, "drop in anytime and I'll take a lesson."

With that Tex scooted outside with a quick *adiós* to the two of them.

"By the way, Bro," said the priest as he watched the boy going up the sandy street, "I come bearing glad tidings. The bishop wants you to go along on a boat trip to Cavinas with Father Considine and myself.

We'll be gone from ten days to two weeks and you'll get to see the country and learn some of the customs of the country people."

Brother Gonzaga was all eagerness. He had been wondering how long he would have to wait to see the places the missioners talked about at night. "When do we start?" he asked.

"Well, Father Considine comes in this afternoon, so we should be able to get off the day after tomorrow. And I've got another surprise for you," he added. "This will be my last trip; from then on you take over the good old *Innisfail.* So keep your eyes open this trip and learn all you can."

"I sure will," Brother promised him, already planning to get down to the river and talk to the mechanic.

Early on the morning that they were to leave for Cavinas, Brother was down at the riverbank of Riberalta. Standing on the edge of the embankment, a hundred feet or so above the river, he let his eyes rove over the scene to get the feel of it. Across the broad expanse of muddy water on the far riverbank, there was nothing but jungle, green and thick and impenetrable. But down below him on this side, there was movement along the shore and on the launches tied up there.

The *Francia,* long, lean and two-decked, was loading. She was so high out of the water and so narrow that she appeared to be ready to tip over. Down in her hold she had a goodly portion of the wood she would need for her trip, and already the huge smokestack was belching black smoke. Alongside, looking like something from the Mississippi's early days, the *Helvetia* with its enormous paddle wheels was unloading, having come in the night before. Several smaller launches, some canoes hollowed out of tree trunks and belonging to the country people, and two of the mission boats with outboards were staggered along the beach. A gang of stevedores had dumped part of the *Helvetia*'s cargo on a small flatcar and were winching it up the rails that led to the top of the embankment. Brother's eye was caught by one of the small boys who were already fishing the river. The tiny figure waved and yelled, "*Buenos días, Hermano.*" Gonzaga recognized his friend Tex and waved back.

In the midst of all this, moored between the *Francia* and the *Helvetia* and looking like a plank of wood with two orange crates fore and aft, was the *Innisfail*.

The *Innisfail* had been given to the mission by Msgr. James Kelly of Jamaica Plains, Massachusetts. She had been shipped down from the States in the hold of a freighter, carried up the length of the Amazon and then taken by railroad (the famous Mamoré-Madeira Railroad) and truck to Cachuela Esperanza; she had finally reached Riberalta on the deck of another launch. It had been a long and hazardous trip, and many greedy hands in many ports had caressed her squat lines, each time taking away a memento of their encounter. When she finally arrived in Riberalta, the *Innisfail* had been stripped of everything except the metal hull and the diesel motor.

Brother Gonzaga went down the steep bank, following steps cut in the red soil, and took one last look at her before going aboard. Up close she looked a lot better . . . thirty-five feet long and ten feet wide, with a cabin up front and one in back and a deep well in the center for the motor. On the roof of the forward cabin was mounted a searchlight and a wobbly crate to hold chickens for the trip. On the rear cabin roof was a barrel of water for showering and washing up.

On board, Ignacio the cook was struggling with two chickens which were tied together by a short string; they kept flapping and cackling all over the motor hatch. Up front, José the engineer was fussing with cables leading from the motor to the steering wheel. Orlando—as befit a Beni pilot—was smoking and watching the whole proceedings with a bored eye, flipping his cigarette overboard and pushing back the dirty peaked hat which was the sign of his trade. "You have come early to check everything, eh?"

Brother made a mock salute to the pilot and grinned. "*Sí, mi señor piloto,* I have come to see that Ignacio has enough food, that José has enough oil and that you have enough cigarettes."

The pilot laughed, already in the act of lighting a fresh cigarette. "Without food," he said, "we can still survive. There is always the jungle and the river. Without diesel oil, things are serious. But there is always the *Francia* to tow us. But Orlando, the great pilot, without cigarettes, this indeed is a tragedy. For Orlando without his little vice cannot pilot."

"Seriously," Brother said, "tell me something about this great talent of yours. What is so difficult about being a pilot? The river is wide and there is little traffic."

José raised his head momentarily from his task and

gave Brother a wink.

Orlando turned to José. "Do you hear that?" he said. "Tell our friend what it is to travel this river!"

"Come, *mi hermanito,*" the pilot continued, not expecting an answer from José, "let me tell you about my trade. You say the river is wide. It is indeed wide, but going upstream it is like following a little path in the jungle. We cannot use the middle of the river because there the current runs strong and the motor will not carry us against it. If you take this launch out there, she will hang in one spot, straining and trembling with exertion, but she will make no headway. If the motor quits from the strain, then . . . *adiós,* my little brother, . . . you go back downstream, twisting and turning and then over the falls. So we sneak along the riverbank, where the current is weaker and where a pilot must keep his eyes peeled for the sunken trees. For a hidden tree trunk can rip off your propeller and once again, *mi hermanito,* you are headed for the falls, unless you can jam her up against a bank.

"A good pilot like your humble servant not only avoids the tree, but he seeks out the *remansos.* These are countercurrents, and once you get in them the going is much easier."

It had never occurred to Charlie that the launch could not be steered without power. He had thought that going downstream with the current they would have enough speed to steer by. Orlando was in the process of explaining this phenomenon when there was a hail from the river bank. Fathers John Considine and Robert Fransen came aboard.

Father Considine was making his first trip to Bolivia, having been sent by the Superior General of Maryknoll to make a visitation of the South American missions. He was a seasoned traveler, however, having visited many other missions around the world at one time or another. Despite his nonathletic appearance, this trip was just another one to be taken in stride. Brother, who had read many of Father Considine's publications, greeted him respectfully, and then turned to Father Fransen, who was already engaged in his preparations for the trip. The priest—known to the local people as Padre Roberto—had taken off his floppy straw hat and was vigorously rubbing a greasy-looking liquid all over his bald scalp and red flushed face.

"Here, Brother," he said handing over a bottle, "try this stuff against the *meriouis.*"

The *meriouis* are small insects that leave a bite like a mosquito but with a small red center which lasts for days. In a matter of minutes they can leave your face such a mass of bites that shaving becomes painful and you are driven frantic with the desire to scratch. Ever since coming down to the river Brother had been fighting them off automatically. Now he took the bottle and rubbed in the insect repellent.

"I remember the first trip I made here," Padre Roberto was telling Father Considine. "I had a bottle of this stuff and I was ashamed to use it. I thought that the river people would think I was a sissy. So I suffered all morning till we hit the first house along the river. A big tough fellow came out and after his salutation, his first words were, '*Padrecito,* did you bring along any of that stuff for the insects?' After that, I practically bathed in it. Once we get moving, the wind will keep them astern of us, and it won't be so bad."

"The worst time for the insects," he added reflectively, "is from four in the afternoon till around nine in the morning. Except for the *tábanos* (the flies) . . . they keep it up all the time. Well, Orlando, let's cast off," he continued jokingly, "and see if we can do it without hitting the *Francia* this time."

José, who was down in the motor pit, let out a guffaw. Orlando, tossing away his cigarette, arranged his cap at a rakish angle, waved to two girls who were watching the proceedings and nonchalantly threw the launch into gear.

The first night they made Ivon, a small pueblo run by the house of Suarez and boasting a small wooden chapel. They had night prayers for a handful of people and Padre Roberto baptized a baby. In the morning they said Mass early and were on their way.

The excitement and the glare of the river had knocked Gonzaga out on the first day. By mid-afternoon of the second day out he was stretched out on the front cabin roof, relaxed and a little sleepy but still watching all the activities around him. Father Considine was down in the cabin fighting the vibration and trying to keep his diary up to date. Brother had been impressed by many things—the chatterings of the parrots overhead; the cranes with their handsome black, white and grey plumage; the apparently aimless course of the innumerable butterflies; the fish that occasionally leaped from the water; the ugliness of a water pig that

Father Fransen had failed to hit with his rifle. But most of all Brother had been struck by the tropical vegetation, the scarcity of people here and the heavy cloak of trees. He was surprised also to see so little game.

Father Fransen was back with Ignacio the cook, arranging for the evening meal and cleaning his twenty-two caliber rifle at the same time. He did not believe in hunting just for the sake of hunting; but he also had no intention of subsisting on tough chicken for the remainder of the trip if he could get in a couple of good shots along the way.

It was wonderful up on the cabin roof in the hot sun, listening as the putt-putt of the motor bounced back off the jungle wall. Brother was half asleep when he heard the sound of the motor change its rhythm to a cough. Orlando shouted something and José dove for the motor pit. Brother clambered down just in time to see Orlando heading for a small sandy beach up ahead.

Despite the excitement and his fear that the motor might kick out altogether, Orlando could not help but try to impress Gonzaga. "Now, my little brother," he said, "you will see how a good pilot acts when there is danger."

Gonzaga smiled and watched the maneuver. Orlando brought the vibrating launch up slowly to the beach inch by inch, so as not to hang her up. Watching the stern so that the current wouldn't catch it, he touched the prow up on the sand as gently as a mother caressing her baby. In a second Ignacio, commandeered from the kitchen, had dropped overboard and hammered a meter-long metal spike into the sand. A line was warped around it, and José cut the motor.

Orlando turned and smiled at Brother as though expecting a thunder of applause. Brother burst into laughter at the gesture. "*Ay, qué talento!* (what a talent!)," he said.

Padre Roberto looked down into the motor well, watching José at work. Father Considine hovered solicitously nearby as Brother Gonzaga passed the necessary tools down to José.

"I just hope," Father Fransen said philosophically and in a resigned voice, "to make a trip in this launch without motor trouble. Just one trip before I die. That's all I ask."

Despite the trouble and the grease and the sweat, José grinned and kept on working. "But when she works, she works well, *no, padrecito?*"

"Sure, when she works. When she is not eating sand in the water pump, when she is not burning out, and when the generator is functioning. Sure, she works well. But tell me, José, since I have been running this boat, when has it happened that none of these things have come to pass?"

"Never, *padrecito*. But have patience. In a few moments she will work well again."

"Okay, José, I quit. I'm going for a swim. Let me know when you're ready. Come on, Brother, grab your suit and let's cool off."

Gonzaga changed into his trunks and dove overboard, careful not to get into the pull of the current. This far up river away from the town the water was clear and cool and refreshing. He could feel it soothing his sunburned face and caressing the *meriouis* bites. Later as he was drying off, the sting came back again, but the moment of relief had been one of pure pleasure.

Aboard, José had the motor functioning again. After a quick dip on his part, they took off, with Padre Roberto piloting and Orlando stretched out asleep on the back cabin. Brother went up forward to keep Father Fransen company.

After a moment Padre Roberto said, "Oh, I forgot to mention it, but you've got to be careful swimming around here. The place is full of *rayos* (stinger rays). They can do an awful job on you."

Gonzaga shuddered. "Thank you so much, *padrecito,*" he said ironically. "I am learning much this trip. Would it be possible to learn some of these things before the knowledge becomes absolutely necessary for my life?"

Padre Roberto laughed and shrugged. "We have so much to learn all our lives down here. It is a continuous process. Just now we are coming up to a little clearing where a man lives all alone with his wife and his young children. He will hear our motor far downstream and will be waiting for us. He will come running from the jungle and signal us to stop. He will want company for a few minutes. To see and hear something of what is happening down in the town.

"I will talk to him and give him some tobacco and I will baptize his newborn if there is one. Then I shall go away depressed, not really knowing him or what he is thinking and feeling. Unable really to get inside him and his loneliness and misery.

"Sometimes I wonder what it is all about. Why has God put them here? Why wasn't I born here instead of in the United States, where I had so many good things, a fine education and a wonderful father and mother?"

"It's just God's Divine Providence, I guess," Gonzaga said. "Maybe He put people here so we could save our souls by helping them."

"Sure, that's part of it, of course," the priest answered. "But sometimes you wish these people could just get a break once in a while. How many hundreds of times have I come up to a little *barraca* with maybe six or seven huts made out of bamboo and up on stilts? I've watched the man come down to the shore, dressed in an old pair of trousers and a tattered shirt. His wife comes out of the hut in an old dress, the kids in little undershirts, all of them covered from head to foot with infected bites from the insects. These people get up in the morning, have a little cup of ersatz coffee made with river water; and when they finish they have a quarter of an inch of mud sediment left in the cup. Then they take a handful of rice and go off into the jungle to tap the rubber trees. They're back home at night to smoke the rubber before their huts. Finally, when they have gathered enough rubber, they sneak it down river and trade it for a few handfuls of sugar and salt and rice.

"Such people are born, give birth and die without ever seeing a doctor and they step off into eternity without the chance of the Last Sacraments. Whew! I better stop, Brother my boy, for I'm beginning to get preachy."

Gonzaga had been absorbed in what the priest was saying. But now he looked up and into the distance. "Padre," he asked, "isn't that a canoe up there, low down in the water and coming fast?"

"You've got good eyes, Bro," Father Fransen said. "Yes, that's a canoe and it's beginning to slow down. Looks like one of the Indians from Cavinas."

The owner of the canoe, however, was not an Indian but Father Ambrose Graham on his way down to Riberalta. Soon they were lashing the canoe to the side of the *Innisfail.* Father Graham had decided to go back up river with them.

CHAPTER 9

They stayed overnight and the next day in Cavinas. Brother spent most of the time on the launch helping to ready it for the return trip. Later he was to spend some time in Cavinas and find it the most interesting place he had ever visited. On the trip down the river on this occasion things went smoothly.

Brother Gonzaga was in the habit of sitting above deck between the two cabins, atop the motor well. Here in turn he meditated, said the Little Office of the Blessed Virgin, and fingered his rosary. He was already accustomed to the idea that a busy missioner does not need a church to say his prayers. A horseback ride, or a trip on a jolting truck or a noisy launch, affords the missioner a chance to meditate and to pray.

On that first day returning down river, he was sitting there listening to the sound of the motor kick back off the solid wall of jungle, when Father Ambrose Graham came along and sat beside him.

"Well, Brother," he asked, "how do you like our little mission down here?"

"Well, Padre, I can't really say. I haven't seen very much yet. But one thing I can say. There is one whole lot of jungle and water in these parts."

Father Graham laughed and lit a cigarette, shielding the lighter against the breeze. "You're right about that," he said. "When I was back in the States I used to complain about all the billboards cluttering up the beautiful scenery. Nowadays, I'd like to see a couple of them on those trees, just to break the monotony. What I'd really like to see, though, is a couple of super-gasoline stations every so many miles."

"That must be a real problem, taking your gasoline along for every trip you have to make. I saw that boat of yours and you didn't have more than an inch of freeboard."

"With all the other equipment we have to carry, it's bad enough," the priest answered, "but with the gas, too, it's almost impossible."

Brother, who had visions of himself getting some priest ready for a similar trip, was eager to learn just what was carried on these visits to the *barraca* people. "Tell me, Father," he asked, "what do you take along with you?"

Father Graham after so many trips had simplified the matter of packing by using a check list. He ran through the items easily. "First of all," he recited, "you break things down into categories. There are foodstuffs, medicines, sacramental things, teaching equipment, and operational supplies. Under foodstuffs you take along a bit of rice and jerked beef just in case you get stuck somewhere with no food. Maybe even a couple of bags of dehydrated soup for a quick lunch when you want to keep moving.

"My medicine chest is fairly simple. A snake bite

kit, a needle and suture, a few instruments and some of the standard remedies like aspirin, epsom salts, atebrin, and two or three other remedies for malaria.

"Under the sacramental things I include the Mass kit, the holy oils, and of course a supply of wine and hosts."

Brother interrupted him, "What happens if you run out of hosts?"

"I make my own," the priest said. "Just get a little pure wheat flour, mix it with some water and bake it. Naturally they don't come out like they were made by a group of Carmelite nuns, but they are valid enough."

Father Graham stretched his legs out and continued. "The teaching equipment takes up a lot of space, but it wouldn't do much good to travel without it. First of all I have a projector for movies and slides, the slides and films themselves, catechisms and some holy cards and medals. To operate the projector I have to carry a 500 watt gas engine to generate electricity, and that is a really heavy item. I have two moving picture films which I show every time, both of them in color; one about the life of Christ, and the other about the Blessed Mother. The slide films are on the Sacraments."

"And finally we come to what I call operational items: gas for the outboard and the generator, a primus stove for quick cooking, utensils, and so on. That about does it, Brother, and when you get all that aboard, you're lucky to be still afloat."

"Whew," Gonzaga breathed, "That's quite a load. How long do you stay in each place?"

"Well, in the beginning I had a tough time. The

administrators of the small *barracas* weren't too happy to see the people take time off, so I had to go wandering through the jungle looking for them wherever they were working the rubber trees. But now after they have seen the pictures and want to be entertained again, I have it easy. They would be apt to manhandle the administrator if he let me pass by without notifying them. So I send word ahead and tell them when I will arrive, and they drop everything for three or four days and are waiting on the riverbank for me. A good time is had by all," he finished laughingly.

"Well," he continued, "you've pumped me dry. If you keep that up with everyone you meet, you'll soon know all there is about things down here. I'm going to get some Breviary said up on the cabin roof. *Hasta luego.*"

The round trip to Cavinas had been a hurried one, taking only ten days, since Father Considine was traveling on a tight schedule. On arrival in Riberalta, Father Considine rested a day or so and took off for Guayaramerim by plane. From there he would travel by truck to Cachuela Esperanza. The plan was for Brother Gonzaga to meet him there with the *Innisfail* and bring him back once again to Riberalta.

Meanwhile Brother went back to his Spanish classes, to reassembling broken down motors and to helping Father James McCloskey with the altar boys, teaching them to serve Mass, and in general acting as counsellor to them.

There were about ten youngsters who were completely faithful, who came around not only for the practice sessions but also to inveigle Brother into leaving his work for a session on the basketball court or a jaunt into the nearby jungle for a little hunting. There was little Tex and Jaimé Ruiz, the smallest of the gang, Alberto Ferrufino and Armando Dominguez, who was big for his age. They could be as sweet as angels or as great a gang of needlers as ever hindered a tired Brother from taking a siesta.

Brother, back in Riberalta only a few days, was in the process of cleaning the water filter of the *Innisfail* when the gang of them appeared in the doorway of his workshop. It was Tex who acted as the spokesman.

"*Hermanito,*" he grinned, speaking slowly so that Brother would get it all, "it is hot in here, no?"

Brother who was drenched in perspiration, was inclined to answer in a strong affirmative, but suspecting a trap answered non-committedly.

"When one works hard, one does not mind the heat, but," and here he made it plain with his stare, "for those who roam the streets with nothing to do but think of mischief, then the day can become very hot. But not as hot as it will be later for such time wasters."

Unabashed Tex continued his appeal. "But, *hermanito,* it is the siesta hour when no one works."

"Except gringos," said a voice from the rear.

"They're crazy," someone else supplied, disguising his voice, and they all giggled.

"And," Tex continued, "the jungle is cool and the birds are sleepy, *hermanito,* and they will sit still for us."

"No can do," Brother said, "*vayanse.* Beat it and

stop bothering those of us who have a conscience."

Tex began to wheedle now. "But, *Hermano,* you promised to let me teach you to use the slingshot."

"Okay," Brother said, turning back to his work, "but not now. When there is time. Maybe after Mass on Sunday."

Tex sneaked up behind him quietly, and without a word deposited a brand new slingshot on the table. It had been worked on with loving care and had taken a lot of time to make.

"I made it myself, *Hermano*. Just for you."

Brother Gonzaga was moved more deeply than he cared to show. It was the first of many small gifts that these poor people were to give him out of affection. He turned and looked at all the young expectant faces.

"Let's go," he said smiling. "A new tool should be broken in quickly."

Tex was right. Inside the jungle it was cool and silent. Nothing moved. It was hard to imagine that the trees high up were full of nesting birds and that the slight underbrush hid all kinds of small animals quietly waiting for the hunters to move on. A bird startled by their approach screeched overhead in short flight. It was dark and somber in woodland. The taller trees reached up a hundred feet overhead and formed a mat of tangled branches that kept the sun from penetrating. They stood silently, peering up into the trees for small game, whispering when it was necessary to communicate, overawed by the silence and the stillness.

Suddenly, Tex gestured to a spot high up on the trunk of a tree. Brother followed his pointing finger but was unable to see anything.

"A lizard," Tex whispered, just as it moved slightly. Brother finally saw it. Tex lifted his slingshot carefully and took aim. There was a slight whir when he released the rubber and then the lizard came falling lightly to the ground.

"*Ole*," Armando whispered, and they all crowded around the animal. It was ugly and warted and quite dead. Brother was amazed at the marksmanship of the little Japanese. Later feeling squeamish about killing even a lizard, he tried his own luck at a cluster of nuts on an alamendra tree, but failed to come even close.

Tex showed him how to hold the weapon. "*Oye, Hermano*," he said, "like this. The thumb so, upright against the base. Don't wrap it around. And the left arm like this . . . straight out, with the elbow stiff. Only the right arm moves to pull back the sling and when you let it go, do it quickly."

Brother tried again and his direction was good, but the ball fell short. "Ah, ah," said the boy, "I forgot to tell you. You must always aim just a little higher, because the ball does not go in a straight line."

With the lesson completed, Brother's marksmanship improved. Before they left the jungle the boys told him that he would soon be as good as they.

Brother Gonzaga left Riberalta to pick up Father Considine on October 3rd, the feast of the Little Flower. He was struck by the coincidences that his first command of the *Innisfail* should occur on the feast day of the saint to whom he was most devoted. He placed the launch under her protection and nailed her picture up in the pilot's cabin.

The trip was a short one and uneventful. They were back in Riberalta the next day in time for the annual retreat of all the priests. The accommodations were poor for the number of men and their baggage. The cots and the mosquito nettings sprawled out into the corridors and Brother Gonzaga, who slept on a cot in his workshop in the chapel building, considered himself lucky to be living in comparative luxury.

At night during recreation period the priests gathered in the dining room and played cards distractedly, glad to have someone to talk to after so many lonely months. The stories they told were tall tales embroidered by imagination and the long planning about just how they were going to tell them when they had the chance. There were stories of encounters with jaguars, and with alligators and snakes, and one told how he had been eaten out of house and home by the soldier ants that march endlessly in a straight line consuming whatever is in their way.

Gonzaga sat back and listened to the talk with delight. It was the first time he had seen all the priests together since he had arrived at the mission. There was Father Gordon Fritz, looking like a slightly shopworn acolyte, with muscles bulging under his T-shirt below his unlined angelic face; Father Thomas Collins, his round face twisted in a perpetual grin, his eyes sparkling with good humor behind his steel rimmed glasses, his T-shirt bulging not with muscles but with a well-rounded stomach; Father Walter Valladon, dark browed, his jutting chin giving the impression of sternness until he chuckled; Father Hilary Jakowski, the "Immaculate Jug" who piloted his launch in white sharkskin cassock, and gold plated cufflinks in his sleeves, and emerged at day's end looking as though he had just dressed for dinner. There were younger men, too, but these priests had been in the mission from the beginning —their stories were funnier and taller, and their joshing slightly more barbed as long friendship and living together gave them this right.

They shouted and laughed uproariously over each play and each sally, tossing incredibly dirty and torn *bolivianos* on the table. The money was practically useless. In fact had they been playing with nails or matchsticks which were valuable and hard to get, they might have been accused of gambling; but the *bolivianos,* smelling of the mold of the tropics, the printed figures long since blurred by sweat and countless handlings, had less value than stage money.

Father Fritz called to Father Tom Collins, his voice breaking in the way that it had when he was excited. "Tell Gonzaga about that famous altar of yours."

Father Collins' grin widened. "The tragedy of my life, Brother," he said, "and they make a joke out of it. They're sadists at heart."

"Come on, Father Tom, tell it again," Father Valladon pleaded. "Brother hasn't heard it yet, and besides," he added chuckling, "it always brings tears to my eyes."

"Okay, okay," Father Tom said, "you won't give up till I do. I was in a place called Fortaleza," he said turning to Brother, "and like everything else in the place, the church was falling apart. There were bats within the wooden walls and hanging from the rafters, and at night when the bats went foraging, the owls came in and took over. I stood it as long as I could, and then I rolled up my sleeves and went to work. After a time I had the church pretty well cleaned up and sealed off with screens, but the altar was beyond repair. So I sat down and designed an altar, figuring everything to the inch. I sent the design down to Riberalta here, where they have a couple of competent carpenters.

"After a couple of months I wrote to ask how things were going and they told me they had never received my letter. So I drew the plans over again, waited two weeks for a launch and sent them down once more. I used to lay awake at night dreaming of that altar—how it was going to be to say Mass on an altar that didn't creak and sway each time I leaned over at the Consecration.

"After six months I made a trip to Riberalta, prepared to take the altar back up with me. Well, you can imagine how I felt when I found the carpenter hadn't even started it. He was making furniture for the townspeople and since they were here to pressure him, and I was far away, he just kept putting off building the altar. I raised the devil with him, of course, and saw him started on it before I went back to my mission.

"In the months that followed I didn't dream any more—you can only keep a dream so long—but I began to hate that old altar of mine, more and more.

"Finally, a year and a half after I had drawn up the original plans, a launch came in and the kids informed me that the altar was aboard. It was late in the evening and getting it off the boat in the dark was a problem. I decided to wait until the morning. I didn't sleep that night for thinking and planning how I was going to set it up. I was still awake at three in the morning when I heard a lot of shouting in the plaza and came out to investigate what was going on. From the doorway I could see a red glare in the sky down by the river. It flared up, then died down; and then flared up and died down, and then flared up again.

"You can guess the rest. By the time I got to the river, the altar had burned to ashes and the launch, burned to the water line, was just sinking in the middle of the river. So good-bye dreams and good-bye altar."

"Wasn't that sad?" Father Valladon laughingly asked Brother. "I knew you would enjoy it."

For a moment Brother was nonplussed, and then he laughed along with them, realizing that these men had long ago learned to laugh at tragedy as means of survival. Without a sense of humor, such disappointments could drive a man inside himself, leaving him a brooding neurotic in a lonely mission station. They had counteracted with the only means at hand . . . laughter. After a while the tragedy was seen in its real light and a man had the courage to start all over again.

As the evening wore on Brother Gonzaga watched and listened to the priests bantering each other. They were men who would try anything once, and frequently their experiments failed. They kidded each other about their failures, taking the sting and the embarrassment out of them by so doing.

"Take old Jim here," Father Collins said. "He started a farm outside of town. Tell us, Jim, what happened to that corn you promised us for the retreat?"

Father Logue laughed at the mention of the corn. "The tractor broke down, the weeds grew up and the bugs ate the corn," he explained, "but I got a nice tobacco crop. How do you like this cigar? Grew it, cured it, and rolled it all by myself."

"Sure," Father Fritz said, "and it has so many holes in it that you have to block them with all ten fingers to get a drag out of it. You look like a piccolo player smoking it."

They were still laughing when someone shouted "duck!" from the next room. They barely had time to fling themselves under the table when a gun went off, reverberating noisily in the close quarters.

Brother Gonzaga was too surprised to move. He was sitting upright in the same spot when the voice came again, "Got him!"

They all filed into the next room to Father Fransen, rifle in hand, standing over a dead rat the size of a small cat. "He came walking along that rafter as big as life," he said, "and when I had to shout to you fellows I thought he would get away."

"The Great White Hunter," someone said. "Some day you're going to miss and goodbye tile roof. But I'm going to sleep better out in that corridor tonight, that's for sure."

When the retreat ended Brother watched them all going back to their missions for another year. It seemed to him that the companionship had done more for them than the retreat itself. After all there were many hours in a quiet jungle town when you could talk to God. There weren't many hours when you could talk to your fellow missioners.

CHAPTER 10

June of 1946 was a hot month in Riberalta. Brother Gonzaga, who was always affected by the heat, had taken off his cassock after everyone had left the sacristy that Sunday afternoon. Dressed in a T-shirt and white trousers, he was busy putting away the vestments that had been used for Mass in the morning. It suddenly occurred to him in the midst of these labors that it was almost exactly a year since he had sat in the hot sun of the quadrangle at Maryknoll to receive his assignment to Bolivia.

It had been a year in which he had learned a lot of new things: a new language which he now spoke fluently, new ways of living, different ways of eating, and a whole new set of friends. He had his routine of prayers and work arranged pretty well now, his Mass and meditation and communion in the morning, his office at noon, and in the evening after work and a cold shower, his Holy Hour before the Blessed Sacrament.

Sometimes he wished that another Brother would be assigned to the mission so that these exercises could be held in common, but for the most part he felt that everything was working out fairly well. He had caught up with most of the work on the motors and on the other odd jobs around Riberalta, and while there was always something popping up, he had a little more time now to devote to the altar boys and the rest of the urchins in town. He had become their friend and confidant, and bike mender for them all, and it was this part of his work that he loved best. He knew boys well, and during his early life in the orphanage he had been thrown among them and learned more about them than the ordinary boys growing up in the States. His years of driving the school bus in Akron had given him an added insight into youngsters. And these lads in Bolivia weren't any different. They wanted attention and affection and someone to take an interest in them.

In the beginning though, he remembered, he hadn't worked it out so well until he had a talk with Father Collins. He had come into the rectory in Riberalta looking as though he were carrying the burdens of the world on his shoulders. The priest had glanced up from his breviary and noticed immediately that something was wrong.

"What's the matter, Bro?" he asked, "did you lose your favorite wrench?"

Brother Gonzaga wasn't one to talk about his problems, but he couldn't help himself this time. "I just sweated for three days over that motor for the small boat. I took it apart, I cleaned it, I worked on it till it sounded like a watch. You know what? That lazy lad who helps around the port was putting it on the boat and dropped it into the river. I've got it back in the shop covered with sand and mud with the whole job to do over again!"

The priest began to chuckle. "I'm not laughing at you nor at your problem, Brother," he said. "I'm just laughing at life in general. We're always knocking ourselves out and getting excited about things, and nine out of ten times all the worry and tears are unnecessary. Take your motor for instance. When you take another look at it, I bet you'll find that it isn't in such bad shape, and that you can clean it up easily. It's not the motor that is bothering you, it is just that you've got yourself worked up in general. You've got to sit down and figure out just what you are doing here."

Brother Gonzaga stopped his pacing up and down and looked at the priest with surprise. "Do you think that could be it, Padre? You mean that underneath, something is griping me and I'm taking it out on the motor?"

"Could be," the priest answered, "think it over for a couple of minutes and tell me if I'm right."

Brother resumed his pacing and after a moment of reflection he said, "I believe that you are right at that. I've been working so hard on those motors and all the other things, that I just haven't had time for anything else. I'd like to do a little more praying, and I'd like to get mixed up with the young boys in town a bit more, more teaching of catechism and what not. I guess that I am beginning to resent all the time I have to put in the workshop."

"That about sums it up, I suppose," Father Collins said, "and the first thing you have to do is to get your mind clear about just what your job is. A Brother down here is a trouble shooter. That's just about what it comes to. You're called on to do just about everything under the sun. If an outboard goes on the blink, you're the man for the job. If the Sisters' plumbing system gets out of whack or their jeep conks out they say, 'call Brother.' If I need someone around the rectory here, you're the first one I think of. So you are the trouble shooter of the mission.

"But that isn't all you are. You're the man behind the priest. If I had to spend all day fixing motors or building a church, I'd never get time for administering the sacraments. And that is what I'm here for. That's my job. You can say to yourself, that every time I administer a sacrament you are present there, because you are the one who frees my hands for the job.

"You remember how it was in the time of the Apostles. They started out preaching the Word and baptizing and then as the little communities grew up they found themselves more and more involved with preparing food and waiting on tables and what not, until finally they had to ordain a group of deacons to do that work. Today we don't have deacons in the Church in that sense, and of course you haven't received any of the sacred orders, but we couldn't get along without you any more than the Apostles could get along without the deacons."

"When you put it that way," Gonzaga said, beginning to smile, "I don't feel so bad about that old motor."

"The second thing you have to figure out is this. You can only work so long in the tropics and after that it begins to take its toll. You can't skip meals down here. You need all the energy you can get, because you burn it up so fast. And another thing you need is recreation. You need the companionship of your fellow missioners. I don't have to tell you about your spiritual life, since you're own Brother's rule is pretty clear about that. Do you think I'm preaching at you?"

"No, Father, I don't. I'm grateful to you for bringing it up. I've gotten into a rut in that shop of mine."

"Tell you what you do," the priest said, "sit down and work out a schedule for yourself and see if you can stick to it. Sometimes you'll be called on for an emergency, but you'll be able to keep to a rule most of the time."

So Brother drew up a schedule that included the three phases of his life, his spiritual exercises, his work, and his recreation. He was kneeling before the altar in the little church, just thinking how fortunate his encounter with Father Collins had been when his thoughts were interrupted by a shadow in the doorway and then the gangling figure of Armando Dominguez. Armando genuflected quickly to the tabernacle, blessed himself in that complicated ritual the South Americans have, ending by kissing the back of his thumb, and then, his duty over for the moment, waved a bathing suit at Brother with one hand and gestured with the other towards the river.

Brother had thought earlier that a nice long siesta this quiet Sunday would be just what the doctor ordered. But when he saw Jaimé Ruiz, Alberto Ferrufino, and little Tex join Armando in the doorway, he decided that he might as well go along.

Outside the sacristy the heat was even more intense

as they walked down to the riverbank. The boys had wet their bathing suits and placed them on their heads, but by the time they came to the river the suits were almost dry again. They found eight more of the boys waiting for them near the canoes and suddenly it occurred to Brother Gonzaga that he was going to have a job on his hands to watch over so many of them. He knew that a couple of them, including Tex and Jaimé Ruiz, couldn't swim very well and the current in the center of the river was quite strong. On the mission side the river had dropped so far that they had to walk some distance over the dried cracked river bed to the water. On the other side, shining in the sun, was a long stretch of sandy beach. In the middle the river flowed swiftly.

He decided to check the boys out. He asked each one of them separately if they had permission to go swimming. When he came to Tex, he saw the boy hesitate, then shake his head in the negative. Brother knew that the boy's parents kept a pretty close watch over him, "Tex, I'm sorry but you can't come along without permission."

"But, *Hermano,*" Tex pleaded, "if I go back for permission you will go off without me."

Brother looked at the eager brown face, contorted now with anxiety, and thought how much he liked this little Japanese kid who had become almost his shadow, helping around the workshop, running errands and in the jungle pointing out the best spots to hunt. *"Corre! corre!* run," he said, "and we will wait." He watched the tiny figure scamper up the steep embankment and turned back to the other boys.

"Armando, you take charge of the second canoe and take the best swimmers with you. I'll take the other canoe with the smaller lads."

They had hardly gotten settled in the canoes when Tex came running back. Out of breath he jumped into the canoe with Brother Gonzaga. They paddled slowly across the river, drifting downstream a bit, and then when close to the other shore where the current was negligible, worked their way back up to the beach. They stuck the paddles in the wet sand and tied the canoes to them with a vine.

They shouted and yelled as their bare feet hit the hot sand. They were out of the jungle seconds later, changed into their trunks before Brother had finished checking the canoes. Gonzaga donned his bathing suit slowly in the dense foliage watching them frolic in the water. He never really enjoyed these trips. It was good to watch the boys enjoying themselves and he enjoyed their affection and confidence in him, but he always felt the weight of responsibility. He was constantly worried that something might happen to them. They were so used to their environment that they were inclined to underestimate the dangers that lurked on all sides.

"*Hermano,*" one of them shouted, "hurry up, we're going to play *piti.*" They had played it before and Brother dashed into the water scattering them on all sides. In this game he acted out the part of the *caiman,* the alligator, diving under water and grabbing them by the legs, careful not to hurt them, but giving them a good ducking just the same. They shouted and squealed and did their best to avoid him.

They were exhausted after an hour or so and dropped on the beach on large leaves they had brought out of the jungle. Brother was always amused at the simplicity of the arrangements. Back in the States people went to the beach with blankets, sun lotion, thermos bottles, beach umbrellas, portable radios, picnic lunches and folding chairs. Here the boys changed in the jungle in a matter of seconds, drank the river water, stretched out on leaves that were cooler than blankets, and found fresh fruits and berries among the trees when they were hungry. It was all so simple and so uncomplicated. He stretched out with them, relaxing now that his charges were out of the water.

They dozed for a while, then someone started a mock fight with the wet sand, flinging it with abandon. In a few minutes they were all involved and Brother himself was plastered with sand. Jaimé, one of the smaller lads, got the sand in his eyes and began to cry. Brother cleaned him up while the rest went back into the water to wash off.

Gonzaga was enjoying a last dip. He was on the verge of calling everyone in to get dressed when there was a frantic shout, "*Hermano, Hermano, ayuda, ayuda!*"

He turned to see three of the younger boys struggling in deep water. Alberto Ferrufino was the closest and Gonzaga started for him at top speed. Just then Alberto got his footing and, breathless, struggled to shore. Brother went on and grabbed Jaimé Ruiz whose pale, scared face was only a few yards away. He dumped him unceremoniously on the sand and turned to see Tex being dragged along in the current. At that moment Armando, a strong swimmer who had raced down the beach, dove in after Tex. Brother scampered up the beach and ran downstream, the wet sand clinging to his feet and holding him back. He could see Armando grab Tex by the hair and hear Tex screaming and struggling. Then Tex disappeared and Armando was alone in the water, fighting his way in against the current. Brother dove in near the spot where Tex had gone down, groping desperately in the murky, muddy water, praying and probing, but his outstretched hands encountered only emptiness. He surfaced, then dove again. Then again and again, till exhausted and half mad, he made it back to the shore assisted by Armando.

Brother Gonzaga had no hope now of finding Tex alive, but after sending Armando back to town for help he continued to dive in the spot where Tex had gone down. Presently all the young men of the town, including the Japanese who were excellent swimmers, joined him. They continued to search until nightfall, then built fires on the beach keeping vigil till the dawn. Brother went back to town and spent the night in chapel on his knees. He wept uncontrollably when he thought of little Tex, how he had first come into the workshop that day with the slingshot in his shy attempt to make friends.

After Mass and communion Brother went back and resumed diving with the others. Twenty-four hours after the drowning, at three o'clock in the afternoon someone on the bank shouted, "There he is!" A canoe with three men in it brought the tiny body to shore. Brother helped them lift Tex out of the water, wrap him in a sheet and take him back to town.

Tex's father, a pagan, collapsed when they brought the body into the house. His mother was hysterical.

Brother stayed with them as long as he could bear the sight of their agony and then he went back to the chapel and spent the next several hours on his knees in prayer. He told himself that it was God's divine will; he remembered that Tex had been to communion that morning and that perhaps if he had lived he would have lost his innocence over the years and quite possibly his soul. He tried to tell himself that he had not been responsible, that it was an accident that could have happened to anyone. And yet he would not be consoled. "I shouldn't have let him come along," he told himself, "I knew he couldn't swim well. I should have checked again when he came back to the canoe, whether or not he had permission." For Tex's mother had been shouting that the boy had never been given permission to go swimming.

They don't keep bodies long in the tropics. There are no facilities for embalming and the law says that the body must be buried before sundown to prevent the possible spread of disease. Mass is said in the church after the burial with a catafalque in lieu of the dead person. Brother Gonzaga, exhausted by his self recriminations washed and changed, stopped by his worktable a moment to pick up an object there and went out to the interment. The whole town was present, and as Brother pushed his way through the group, many murmured little consolatory words to him.

"*No te preoccupes,*" they said to him, "*era su destino.* Do not fret, it was his destiny." And so they summed up their philosophy of life in an attempt to lessen his sorrows. They lived a hard life, beset with sickness and accidents, poverty and revolutions, and they had come to accept everything with a fateful shrug of the shoulders. If a man drowned in the river, it was his destiny; if a woman died in childbirth, it was her destiny too. It was their favorite phrase in their songs and in their conversations.

Brother numbly nodded his thanks to them and finally stood at the grave beside the mother and father of little Tex, watching Father Gallagher, the pastor of Riberalta, give the last blessing. The immediate relatives of the boy were sobbing uncontrollably as was the custom among these people, and the words of the service could hardly be heard above the weeping. At last, when Gonzaga thought he could bear it no longer, they lowered the rough hewn casket into the grave. Father Gallagher shoveled in the symbolic first bit of dirt and the relatives dropped the sweet smelling jungle flowers on top. There was a silence then, and Brother felt that all eyes were upon him. He looked around slowly at the tearful faces. Stepping forward he reached into his cassock pocket. He took out the slingshot that Tex had given him, held it momentarily in the hot sunlight and then dropped it into the grave. He didn't wait for the rest of the ceremony. He hurried back to his room and flung himself on his cot, cassock and all, the hot tears welling up.

When Father Gallagher came back from the cemetery he looked into Brother's room. Gonzaga was still stretched out on the bed, murmuring one phrase over and over again. Father Gallagher came up closer to hear what he was saying. "Never again, never again," he kept repeating.

Father Gallagher who himself had been so moved by the tragedy that he could not bring himself earlier to visit the house of Tex, thought that he knew what Brother was going through. He sat down on the bed and began to massage Brother's neck with his long fingers.

After a few minutes Gonzaga rolled over, blew his nose and said vehemently, "Never again will I let one of these people get inside me. It hurts too much. That kid was like a little brother to me."

"I guess we've all said that at one time or another, Brother," the priest said. "We've all made the same promise. You come down here fresh and eager and zealous, wanting to love these people and to devote your life to them. You go into a little town, and you're lonely at first and then someone comes around shyly with a grapefruit or a chicken; and then another one comes, trying to show you how much they appreciate your being there; and then all at once you know everyone in town is your friend, and in many ways they have taken the place of the family and friends you have left behind. Then you are changed to another town. They come out on the riverbank and watch you leave and the kids look at you kind of funny as though you were deserting them and some of the women begin to cry softly. The men try to make jokes about it, but you know that they feel it just the same. You try to keep up a bold front as the launch pulls away, but all the way down the river you keep telling yourself it's the last time you'll leave a hunk of your heart behind.

"But there never is a last time, thank God. You go on to the next town and the next, and after awhile you realize that God has given a missioner a special kind of heart. You grow a new piece for all the pieces you leave behind."

Brother, dry eyed, was watching him now, and Father Gallagher thought he had understood enough for the time being. He slapped him roughly on the shoulder and got up to leave. "Get some sleep now, Bro," he said not unkindly, "and don't let me see your face before ten o'clock in the morning. That's an order. I'll say Mass late and you can serve me."

When he had gone, Gonzaga too exhausted to think about what the priest had said, his emotions spent for the moment, rolled over and fell asleep.

Two weeks after Tex's drowning, Brother Gonzaga went up to the Center House in Cochabamba for his annual vacation. It was a pleasure to be in the mountains after the jungle heat, and to forget about motors for awhile. Not that he could completely forget them, for he spent a great deal of his time running from store to store buying the spare parts that could not be bought in Riberalta. Gradually as the days wore on the hurt grew less, till finally he was able to see that the accident had not been his fault. The sorrow found a hidden spot down deep in his being, coming to the surface only once in awhile now, when he saw a lad like Tex playing in the street, or when he saw the same expression mirrored on the face of a boy who stopped him in the street and asked him for a holy card.

About this time he wrote a letter to Bishop James E. Walsh, the Superior General, and he refrained from mentioning the incident:

> Pardon me for not writing sooner. It is nearly a year now since I came to Bolivia and the time just flew by. I hope I have been a help. I like the work and the people a lot. I am here in Cochabamba for my vacation and am anxious to get back to Riberalta. I have enjoyed the change. The scenery here is beautiful. My health has been good, thanks to God, and I hope I can labor for many more years. The Fathers and Sisters are doing marvelous work and the people like them very much. All in the Pando seem to be doing fine and it is a privilege to be here. I keep the coming Chapter in my prayers, also the work of Maryknoll everywhere. God bless you and keep you.
>
> In Jesus and Mary, Brother Gonzaga.

The Chapter of which Brother speaks was held at Maryknoll in August, 1946. Delegates of the missioners came from all over the world to elect a new Superior General and his council, and to formulate new policies for the future. Bishop Raymond A. Lane from Manchuria was elected the Superior General, and Brother, back in Riberalta at the time, wrote him the following letter:

> Congratulations and assurance of prayers. It is about a year since I came to Bolivia and I like it very much. Right now it is very hot and we are busy at present hauling bricks and

adobes for a new school. The people are very friendly. Tonight next door there is a movie called "Mrs. Miniver," outside of that the people don't have much entertainment. We play basketball once in awhile with the young fellows. Little by little the people are coming in due to the fine work of the padres. God has been very good to us, and we hope to be grateful in return by trying a little harder to spread His love. Asking God to bless you, and assuring you of my daily prayers.

Very respectfully in Jesus and Mary, Brother Gonzaga.

Brother's second retreat in Riberalta was conducted by Father E. McCarthy, O.S.A., later Dean of the School of Arts at Villanova, then on a study assignment in Latin America. The main topic of conversation during the recreation periods centered around the new Superior General. He was due to arrive sometime during the retreat for his first visitation of South America. Few of the priests had ever met him personally and guesses as to the strictness of his nature and what he would think of the work were rife.

When he arrived, Bishop Lane turned out to be one of the kindest and most unassuming men who had ever put foot in a mission. He had a tremendous fund of stories and kept everyone howling with laughter. In a very short period of time the priests and particularly Brother Gonzaga came to look on him as a father. He was interested in the missioner's mechanical work, asking Brother innumerable questions about the motors, which were the best for a particular type of river and whether inboard or outboard was preferable. The two of them took to walking around the plaza in the cool of the evening, discussing these things. Brother may have been shy about expressing certain opinions about theological matters but when it came to motors he had no peer.

"What we need, Bishop," he said earnestly, "is a couple of good boats with diesel stationary engines. The outboards are okay, but they cause a lot of trouble. You snag a floating log and the pin breaks or even a propeller. And if you get a big one they eat up gas and down here you have to carry all your gas for a trip with you. That means small boats, and as a result the Fathers are cramped on the boat and out in the sun all day. It is tough enough traveling the rivers for weeks at a time without doing it that way. I'm convinced that we need bigger boats with diesel inboard motors like the *Innisfail.*"

"But Brother," Bishop Lane said, trying to needle him a bit, "here you have the *Innisfail,* which is what you say we need more of, and yet you can't get it in shape to take me up to Cavinas. How do you account for that?"

Gonzaga made a face and shook his head. "I'm sorry about that, Bishop, but it just couldn't be helped. We have been having a lot of trouble with the pump and I just wouldn't want you to get stranded up there."

"But wouldn't you have the same trouble with the other boats?"

"No, Bishop, I don't believe so. It's true that the pump on this type of boat is delicate and these rivers are full of sand that gets sucked into the apparatus, but with a little care we can handle that okay. You see, with the *Innisfail* most of our trouble has come from the fact that the motor was never properly centered. By the time we figured that out we had got a lot of uneven wear throughout, and now one thing after the other keeps happening."

They had made several rounds of the plaza by this time and Bishop Lane still had several interviews with the others to make before leaving on the morning plane.

"Brother," he said, "write me a report on what you have told me and I'll see that something is done about it. In the meantime get that old *Innisfail* in shape. I'll be back again some day and I'm going to want to make that trip with you."

Gonzaga had already prepared some notes on motors for Bishop Escalante to present to the Chapter some months before. Now he sat up half the night developing them for Bishop Lane by the light of a kerosene lantern.

Despite the fact that he had lost a couple of hours of sleep, Brother was up early the next morning to serve the Masses of Bishop Lane and Father McCarthy, who was leaving with the bishop. In the early morning darkness, Bishop Lane celebrated Mass by the light of a kerosene lantern and the candles on the altar. When he had finished Gonzaga started out to the altar with Father McCarthy. They had just entered the sanctuary from the sacristy when Brother suddenly thrust the priest to one side with a quick, "Don't move." Momentarily startled into immobility, the priest watched Brother look around searchingly and then dash to the altar and grab the crucifix there. In one sweeping motion Brother had thrust the pointed end of the crucifix into an object at the foot of the altar and stepped swiftly back. On approaching, the priest saw what had caused the quick action. Still writhing on the floor, but now transfixed by the crucifix behind the head, was a *jo-paro-jo-bobo,* one of the deadliest snakes in the region.

Later in telling the story, Father McCarthy said, "Brother probably saved my life. In the darkness there he looked for all the world like St. Michael the Archangel."

After breakfast the whole community saw the bishop off at the airport. Later coming back to town, Father Thomas Collins nudged Father Gallagher, "Do you see what I see?" he asked. Up ahead of them Brother was walking around surrounded by a bunch of small fry. They were laughing and shouting and trying to trip each other up.

"I sure do." Father Gallagher said, "and he's the one that said 'never again will I let them get close to me.' "

They had come up behind Brother by this time and he turned around grinning. "Okay," he said, "I heard you. Go on, rub it in."

"Just wanted to say that I told you so," Father Gallagher answered, and tripped up Armando Domingues as he went by.

CHAPTER 11

The mission of Cavinas was first opened by the Jesuits in 1756, but the buildings quickly fell into disrepair when the priests were forced to leave soon after the foundation. In 1784 the Franciscans revived the mission. Its center was moved several times within the same general area, the moves necessitated by the proximity of hostile pagan tribes whose presence represented a threat to the Cavinas Indians in their new-found faith. It was only in 1890 that the mission was located at its present site. Franciscan priests were in charge of the mission until 1942 when Maryknollers took over the Vicariate and the mission. The first Maryknoll pastor was Father Ambrose Graham, and later when he was moved, he was succeeded by Father Gordon Fritz who had been his assistant for some time.

The mission is essentially an Indian reservation, the administration of which is entrusted by the national government of Bolivia to the Church, or more properly speaking, to the priest appointed to the area by the Vicar Apostolic of the Pando. The area it covers is a huge tract of jungle and pampa of 170,000 acres, plus another 70,000 acres of ranch land not immediately adjoining. In the jungle area there are many wild rubber trees, a product that has so often proved the boon and the bane of this section of Bolivia. Rubber used to be the main resource of the mission, the money crop, but the market for natural rubber is becoming almost a thing of the past. Brazil nuts are gathered for export, as are the almond-shaped chocolate beans which, like the brazil nuts, are encased in a large outer shell growing directly from the trunk of the tree. Coffee and other crops are also cultivated and in addition the land grows many edible fruits such as mangoes and papaya.

Brother Gonzaga had made many trips to Cavinas. Here he had learned so much about the improvisation of people living in primitive conditions, and it was here also that he met some of the biggest challenges to his mechanical ingenuity in making something out of nothing.

His first trip up river to Cavinas had been made with Father John Considine, but on that occasion he had had no chance to explore the mission. His first big chance came on the Feast of the Solemnity of St. Joseph, April 6, 1948. Instead of using the *Innisfail*, he went along with Father Gallagher on one of the native launches. Father Gallagher was on his way to Fortaleza, loaded down with all kinds of packing cases containing foodstuffs, altar linens, medicines and what not. Brother was practically unencumbered, carrying only a couple of changes of clothing and his kit of tools.

After they had gotten the boxes safely aboard, the two travelers stood on the shore talking to Bishop Escalante, getting last minute instructions and waiting for the launch to sound its whistle. Suddenly with a shrill blast of the whistle and a quick heave of a rope, the launch began to move away from the bank. Caught flat-footed Father Gallagher and Brother Gonzaga made a mad dash for the bank, jumped into one of the launches still tied up, ran its length and grabbed for the *Fortleza* as it glided past. Breathless, they clambered on board, and their first impulse was to throttle the captain. But when they heard Bishop Escalante's laughter from the bank, they calmed down and began to see the funny side of it.

"Did you ever know it to fail?" Father Gallagher asked. "This launch has been sitting here for two days and nights loading a cargo that anywhere else in the world could have been put aboard in six hours, and then suddenly it takes off with two seconds of warning."

"Maybe the captain thought that two days was enough time for anyone to get aboard if he wanted to," Brother said smiling. "Anyway we made it, and that's the important thing."

"Come to think of it," the priest said, "at the rate we are going, we could have walked up the riverbank and caught it at the first stop." He looked over the side and saw another launch full of cargo lashed to the side. From the stern trailed several canoes, and there was even a small gasoline launch hooked on for travel in shallow waters. "This is going to be a real fast trip," he said ironically, and turned around to see the captain coming toward them.

A tall thin Bolivian, almost as tall as Father Gallagher, he walked with that self-assured grace that many foreigners relate to laziness, but which is innate to people who have learned to live by their own resources and who know that in the end patience will bring about all things. They refuse to become excited about the minor things that keep ordinary mortals in constant anxiety.

"Ah, ha . . . *padrecito*," he said smiling, and fingering his hairline mustache, "you almost let us go without you." The priest reflected a moment on the vagaries of the Spanish language. With its use of the impersonal and the reflexive it almost invariably permits throwing the blame on something inanimate, or as a last resort, on someone else. If a cook drops a plate she says, "*el plato se quebro*" meaning, "the plate broke itself," thus taking herself out of the picture quite nicely, and damning the plate irrevocably. It occurred to the priest that they had not let the launch go, but that the launch had left them behind. But long ago he had come to the conclusion that pointing this out would result only in a hurt look on the face of his captain and little satisfaction for himself. So he smiled and agreed with the captain, and used another tactic. "You are right, *mi capitan*," he said, "but it would not have been a tragedy. We could have caught you by swimming. Never have I seen a launch so loaded and so slow in the water. You will be able to retire after this trip."

The captain chuckled realizing that they had embarked on a type of repartee so dear to the Latin heart, where everything is said in a roundabout way, getting a point across, of course, but never by saying it directly. The first man to get angry loses the battle.

The lanky master of the *Fortleza* hitched his trousers with his elbows and stood staring off at the jungle, phrasing his next attack carefully. "A slow trip, *mi Padre,* means more meals for the passengers; more meals means less profit. They will eat my launch out from under me."

The padre began to laugh. "If I know you, you bandit, you have only enough food on board for a day or so. We will be scrounging all over the place for fruit and chickens, and paying out of our own pockets, to keep from starving to death."

The captain shrugged and grinned, "One cannot be blamed for underestimating the number of passengers. There are some," he said slyly, "who come aboard at the last minute."

"You know very well," the priest said, "that we were coming aboard. My boxes have been sitting here for two days. Oh well," he added thoughtfully, "we will find something, I guess, and the most important thing we do have . . . American cigarettes." He knew this last would have an effect on the captain, for there are few of the river people who can resist the idea of smoking *un chester,* as all American cigarettes are called.

"Now, now padre," the captain responded quickly, "we have had our joke, no? There is always enough food for such distinguished guests, and," he added magnanimously, "you must be my guests at the captain's table. I will not take no from you. You will sit with me and that is that."

The priest, who would have preferred to sit with the jungle people, acquiesced, mostly because Brother had farther to go than he, and he was afraid that he might have trouble later on getting food. So he offered the captain a cigarette and went forward to see about hammock space for the night.

As they threaded their way through the baggage and the other passengers to the front of the launch, Father Gallagher nudged Gonzaga and laughed, "Don't get the impression, Brother, that we are fighting. We are really very good friends, but if I let him get away with it, he would have us out there paddling this thing up river."

As it turned out it was the slowest trip ever made in the memory of the captain. The trip to Ivon, the first stop, usually took five hours. They made it in thirteen. On the tenth day they had not yet made Fortaleza, and Brother was over two weeks getting to Cavinas.

At night the passengers slung hammocks from any available spot, sleeping over and under, and in between each other. There was not much need for mosquito netting while the launch was moving, for the breeze kept the mosquitoes away. But on the occasions when they had to stop to buy food or load up on wood, they came aboard in hordes and made life miserable.

Father Gallagher, an old hand at river travel, made himself at home. He showed Brother how to sling his hammock way up in the prow where the breeze was cool and the passengers few. In the early morning hours it can actually get cold on the river, and he taught Brother the trick of putting a blanket under him in the hammock. "Don't worry about what you have on top," he told him, "the sides of the hammock will break the wind; but when it flows under you, it bites right through the canvas and into your back. So get the blanket under you."

They found that they could buy food at the frequent stops, and loaded up with oranges, lemons, limes and tangerines for the long thirsty hours. The captain in a fit of generosity bought bananas, fowl and game whenever he could, but the cook had a genius for making chicken, turkey, duck, venison, beef and fish taste all the same. This may seem at first thought to be a difficult thing to do, but if you boil everything in the same muddy river water, for the same number of interminable hours, in the same dirt encrusted buckets, and put the resultant mess over the same unvarying uncooked rice, it takes no particular talent.

But Father Gallagher and Brother ate it all with good appetite, sprinkling everything liberally with the ever present hot pepper sauce. "They call this stuff *sangre de diablo*" he told Brother (when after a particularly strong dose of it, he began to grow red and to sweat profusely), "which being translated means 'blood of the devil,' and believe me they really hit it on the head with that one."

At night they held songfests aboard the launch. The people were delighted to have something to do after dinner was finished and the long dark night had set in. They sat there in the yellow light of the hurricane lanterns, their open, toothless mouths looking like so many little red caverns in the shadows, and poured their hearts out. "When we are sad, we call on you," they sang.

Later when they had become more friendly, Father

Gallagher passed out some bible histories he had brought along for the occasion. "These people see a priest so seldom," he said to Brother Gonzaga, "we have to take every opportunity to instruct them. And heaven knows we not only have a captive audience here, but a bored one, looking for anything."

The captain looked on it all with an indifferent eye and puffed on one of the *chesters* the padre had given him. He even allowed the use of the one serviceable table for an altar. Brother set the altar up each morning, arranging blankets and hammocks against the wind. The people assisted faithfully, intrigued by the novelty of having Mass aboard a launch.

After Father Gallagher left the launch at Fortaleza, Gonzaga kept up the songfests, but his knowledge of the Spanish hymns was limited and the parties broke up earlier. He sat for awhile then, watching the merchants play gin rummy. There were four of them grouped around a circular table which surrounded the center pole of the launch. The passengers had already strung their hammocks and were swaying gently in the darkness outside the rim of light cast by the lantern on the table. Along with Brother, the captain and two or three of the river people watched the progress of the play. Gonzaga who understood most games of chance, had difficulty following the version they were playing of gin rummy.

Except for the occasional sigh of the fattest of the four players, the silence was broken only by the wheezing of the kerosene lamp and the sound of the motor. Brother was amazed at the incredible smoothness and dexterity with which they fingered the cards and stacked the dirty old bills. These men who traveled the rivers, trading with the jungle people, spent half their lives playing some form of cards in launches and small huts in the jungle.

The little, thin, malaria-yellow gambler with the hairline mustache, finally yawned and stood up. "Thank you, my friends," he said, "I leave the launch during the night and I need a few hours sleep."

The others looked inquiringly at the captain who shook his head negatively and then turned to Brother. "What do you say, *Hermano*, how about a few games?" the fat man asked smilingly.

Gonzaga hesitated a moment, wondering if a refusal to play would be interpreted as not wanting their company, and then shook his head. "No, *gratias*," he said, "I do not understand your game, *amigos*." But those at the table accepted his statement at face value and started a three handed game. With a sigh of relief, Brother watched a while longer and then found his hammock. In the darkness he listened to the click of the cards as the gamblers continued long into the night. He was awakened at six A.M. by the blast of the launch whistle.

"We have arrived," the captain shouted. "*Gratias a Dios, sin novedad.*" It had indeed been a routine and uneventful trip as the captain said.

Brother Gonzaga clambered up the steep riverbank and looked anxiously for someone to meet him. He stared at the small clearing, at the eight or nine lean-tos made out of small tree trunks and leaves, and suddenly realized that no one had come for him. He went back on board and found his kit of tools. Shifting the heavy weight from one hand to the other, he began the long walk to the mission.

The small clearing gave way to solid jungle wall on each side of the road and presently after crossing a deep ravine, he came to a large pasture with a wire fence, and here the road was closed off with a gate. He stood undecided for a moment, looking out over the open ground and marveling at the abundance of ant hills that rose up all over the place. Then he gave his attention to the gate. It was of the type seen all over South America, but it was the first time that he had seen one close up. It was made of horizontal poles attached at one end to a hinged board so they could swing outwards. At the other end another board on hinges fitted snugly against them, holding them in place. This board could be fitted with a lock to keep unauthorized persons from opening the gate. Gonzaga puzzled over it awhile. After examination he figured out by releasing the locking board (which fortunately had no lock attached) he could squeeze through. He closed it again carefully behind him.

Brother walked through the pasture for almost a mile until he came to a small rise, and having breasted it, came into view of the mission itself. The first thing he saw was the tower of the small church and then the other buildings, forming an irregular square around it.

He heard the clanging of the church bells, and saw a short, stocky figure in a white cassock standing in the church doorway. The figure saw him at the same time and waved excitedly.

Father Gordon Fritz, his young, unlined face now creased with smiles came running up to him and extended his hand. "Am I ever glad to see you, Brother," he said. "We never heard the whistle of the launch or I would have met you at the port."

Gonzaga put his tools down and shook hands. "They told me, Father," he said, "that you have a tractor that needed a doctor and here I am."

"It doesn't need a doctor, it needs a surgeon," the priest replied. "I'm afraid that you will really have to operate."

"We'll have a look at the patient as soon as possible," Brother said, "that is, as soon as we have Mass and breakfast, unless," he added anxiously, "I'm too late for Mass?"

"No Brother, I'm just about to begin. After you wash up you can serve."

Later seated on the back porch of the rectory over a breakfast of eggs and a thin slice of beef, Brother sat back, loosed his belt and said, "Man, that's the first decent meal I've had in what seems like ten years."

"Well, Brother, we don't do too badly here, considering that practically everything we eat and use is home-prepared or home-made. We have our own cattle and chickens, our own carpenter shops, brick-making kilns, and just about everything you can think of. I have often thought that the rest of the world could wipe itself out tomorrow and we could go on living here and never know it. Finish up your coffee and I'll show you around."

Brother was restless when he had a job to do. He kept thinking of the tractor, and thought of letting the sight-seeing trip go to later. He thought better of it, and let Father Fritz show him through the rectory. Of the three rooms that faced on the plaza, one was a reception room, another the room of the pastor, and the third a guest room. The priest brought Brother to the guest room first. "This is where you bunk," he told him, "and you don't have to worry about mosquito nets since the screens on the windows are pretty good." Pointing to the huge urn in the corner, he said, "That's your water supply in the *cantaro*. I'll have someone fill it before noon. You just use the dipper to fill the wash basin."

Brother stood staring at the gigantic baked-clay pot the priest had called a *cantaro,* and at the dipper which was made out of a dried gourd. "Thank heavens I don't have to lift that thing," he thought and turned to inspect the rest of the room. It contained a bed that looked fairly comfortable, clothes closet, and several cedar chests. A small desk and a straight backed chair completed the furnishings, with the exception of a kerosene lamp on the desk.

The pastor's room was exactly the same except for a bookcase crammed with books and papers littering the desk. "Right behind your room," Father Fritz said, "is a small dispensary and then the kitchen and a storeroom. As you can see we have no dining room so we eat our meals on the back porch."

At this moment a cart, bringing the rest of Brother's things and the mission supplies from the launch, pulled up in front. In the excitement of unloading Brother managed to grab his tools and find the tractor out back. By noontime, when the priest had finished checking all the things delivered by the boat, and remembered his visitor, he found him at work. The tractor was already taken apart and spread all over the ground. Brother seeing the priest, begged off from lunch with the excuse that he could never remember where all the pieces went if he stopped now. By one-thirty he had it reassembled and ready to crank. For half an hour he and an Indian helper cranked like fury, but the motor refused to turn over. Finally the priest had to intervene.

"Brother," he said, "if you don't stop and rest, you'll pass out. Come on let's have some lunch and a little *siesta* and then you can come back."

"Okay," he answered, "but I'm sure that if I can get a couple of gallons of clean gasoline and wash the rust off all the parts we'll have it going by tonight."

At four o'clock the priest went to see if Brother was still napping. It didn't surprise him to see that the bed had never been used, nor did it surprise him to find Brother under the tractor again. At six-thirty that night he heard the roar of the motor and came out to see Gonzaga grinning in joy. "It wasn't in as bad shape as you thought," he said. "Just rusted up here and there." The priest shook his head in wonderment. To his knowledge no one in all of Bolivia had ever dismantled a tractor twice in one day, and had it working at that!

After dinner they sat smoking on the back porch, listening to the small sounds of the people as they moved around the plaza. "The reason I need the tractor, Brother, is that I have a load of rubber to bring in and get ready for shipment down river. We're going to have to start the day after tomorrow even though the roads are in bad shape."

"How far out is the rubber?" Brother asked absent-mindedly.

"Seventy-five miles," the priest answered, smiling in the darkness.

Gonzaga gulped, "Seventy-five miles! Are you kidding?"

"I knew that would surprise you, Brother, but that's the truth. That darn stuff is seventy-five miles away and we have a couple of rivers to cross in addition."

It suddenly dawned on Brother what he had let himself in for. "You mean we are going to take that tractor seventy-five miles across two rivers and through the jungles; and seventy-five miles back again, with a load of rubber?"

"That's just what I mean, Brother. And not only that but we are going to have three oxcarts behind it full of goods for the people on the way out."

Gonzaga just shook his head at the thought of it. "And furthermore," the priest said, "we are probably going to have to build at least one bridge."

Brother groaned. "Tell me," he asked, "just how long will all this take?"

"Well, I figure it will take a week out and five days back; say two weeks all told."

When Brother didn't answer, the priest burst into spontaneous and uproarious laughter.

"What's so funny about two weeks on a trip like that?" Gonzaga asked, thinking of all the things that could go wrong with the tractor.

"I'm just picturing your face a few moments from now. That's only the first trip. We have to make three of them!"

Brother had nightmares during his sleep, but by morning he was beginning to think the trip might be kind of an adventure at that.

They worked all day loading the carts. Father Fritz had already made up a list of what was needed, so the loading went fast. Back and forth they went from the store to the oxcarts and by noon, with the help of the Indians, they had loaded bolts of cloth, shotgun shells, machetes, tools, and staple foodstuffs, such as salt, sugar and flour.

The store was a short distance from the rectory, a one-story building divided into two parts, the back room being a storeroom. As Father Fritz dragged the goods from the back and flung them on the long counter that ran the length of the store, he explained to Brother. "We have all this stuff brought in on the launch, and we open the store at regular times and sell to the people. They pay for it in work hours, if they are on a building detail here in town, or with rubber, if they are working in the jungle. Then we sell the rubber down river and bring in more goods. Any profit that is made is used for building better homes for the people and taking care of them in general.

"When we first arrived here things were in pretty bad shape. The people had no way of getting necessities unless they traded with the merchants who travel the rivers. They were practically skinned alive by the traders. Right now I would say that they are better off than the people living in the towns."

Brother, who had seen the poverty that existed in some of the tiny *pueblos,* was inclined to agree with him. He looked around at the squat, flat-faced Indians who were transporting the goods and said, "Well, they sure look healthy."

"They are healthy," the priest said proudly, "and what is more they are happy."

CHAPTER 12

The oxcarts which the missioners had loaded were of the common type seen all over the Oriente of Bolivia—a planking of boards on an axle supported by two huge solid wooden wheels. The wheels were made of mahogany, and their size depended on the circumference of the tree from which they had been sliced. Stakes of wood were attached to the planking to hold the goods in place, and the wheels were secured by small wooden pegs thrust through the outer side of the axle. A shaft for the oxen stuck out in front, but for the jungle trip this had now been shortened for attachment to the tractor. Many an oxcart man has been comforted on his long lonely trips by the "song of the wheels," for the huge ungainly wheels warp from side to side as the wagon moves, giving out a rhythmic wood-on-wood rubbing sound that can be heard for great distances in the quiet of the jungle.

Father Fritz had some last minute instructions and some paper work to do, so Brother made a last check on the tractor and then wandered around the little town. The church, made of adobe and roofed with tile, took up one side of the small plaza. Inside the church Brother studied the ornate hand-carved cedar altar and the homemade pews of mahogany and cedar, said a few prayers for a safe trip, asking the protection of the Little Flower in particular. Then, outside again, he turned to the right hand side of the plaza, passed the rectory and the store and came to the carpenter shop. He didn't go in for fear of disturbing the routine of work this last day Father Fritz would be around. He wandered behind the shop instead to peer at the pit where they sawed the huge logs, at the long hollowed out tree trunk used for tanning, and at the brick kilns.

Most of the houses in the plaza were one-room adobe structures with thatched roofs. To this one room was attached a lean-to, open to the elements, where the people were accustomed to cook and to sit and talk.

Brother went to bed early that night while Father Fritz worked late at his desk. When morning came, hot and sultry, Gonzaga felt himself looking forward to the trip. If only that gnawing pain in his stomach would stop, he thought, everything would be perfect.

They got off to an early start, with the roar of the tractor drowning out the creak of the axle wheels and with the two Indians from the town walking alongside balancing the long cedar boards that were to be used to repair the first bridge.

Brother discovered that this bridge was not actually a bridge at all, but a raft made of cedar planking placed over empty barrels. Everything was to be loaded on this, including the tractor, and poled across the Santa Maria river which at this season was about one hundred and fifty feet wide. It took them till late afternoon to repair the raft with the board they had brought, binding it with vines that they had cut from the jungle. They ferried the carts and their contents across safely and then Brother, with some apprehension, eased the tractor down the muddy bank and onto the raft.

They poled frantically against the current and reached the right spot on the other side, but there their luck ran out. As Brother was easing the tractor off the raft, one of the boards gave way and the tractor began to topple. Gonzaga made a leap and landed safely on the raft, but the tractor continued to slide and ended up a few feet from the bank, resting on its side in three or four feet of water.

After a quick glance had assured him that no harm had come to Brother, Father Fritz laughed and said, "Now, Brother, you know why that tractor gets so rusty."

They had it upon the bank shortly with the help of some soldiers to whom they had previously given a lift, and after drying out and wiping off the essential parts, they started out again. They spent the night out on the *pampa,* bone tired, and shivering from cold and exhaustion.

The second day they reached the Viata without mishap and were glad to see that the river was low and only about sixty feet in width. They waded through it without the need of building a raft, and traveled the rest of the day without incident. When they camped out the second night Brother felt less tired and knew that his muscles were becoming accustomed to the sway of the tractor and to the walking when he was spelled by Father Fritz.

They had brought along enough prepared food for the first day, but now they were down to *charqui* for the evening meal. This is a form of jerked beef, sliced into thin strips from the shoulder meat of a steer. The important thing in preparing it is to slice the strips just as one would make a continuous peeling of an orange without nicking it in the process. The strips are soaked in brine and then hung up to dry in the sun. After about three days it is taken down, soaked in water till all the salt is out. The result is a tough but edible meat that needs no refrigeration on long journeys. If by chance the meat becomes infested with maggots, it is merely exposed to the sun till they drop out, and then it is boiled once more.

Brother who was attributing his stomach pains to colic, thought it better to pass up the tough meat and concentrate on a gruel of rice and gravy. They sat smoking afterward, and listened to the quiet rustlings as the small night animals roamed the *pampa*. The two Indians were already dozing a short distance away.

Brother shuddered and the priest looked at him inquiringly. "The whole time we were trying to lift that tractor out of the river yesterday, I kept thinking of those small fish that can strip you to bone in a matter of minutes. I could almost feel them getting closer. What do you call them?"

"Piranhas."

"Yes, those are the ones. Do they really go for you?"

"Usually they don't bother you unless you have a cut and they smell blood. In some places where a big herd of cattle must cross a river, the drovers cut the throat of a cow and dump the carcass into the river. Then while the piranhas work on it, they lead the other cows safely across. Those piranhas leave a skeleton in less than twenty minutes."

After a long silence he continued, "There are a lot of good edible fish in the rivers, though. Maybe when we get back from this trip we can take a day and do some fishing. There's one called the *pairaiba,* about fifteen feet long or so. It lies in the cataracts flapping its tail to keep itself in position and waits for food to come down the river. The people go out in their canoes and sneak up behind it quietly, praying that it won't turn around and slash them with its tail, and then they thrust a javelin into it. They have a line attached to the javelin and attached to the line is a long piece of bamboo. When the fish is struck it takes off down river at great speed. The fishermen follow along slowly, waiting for the *pairaiba* to tire. Eventually they spot the piece of bamboo and know that it is dead. It takes a gang of men to lift it up the bank and the whole town has a fiesta of fish. Sometimes they preserve it by slow roasting and eat it later."

"Well, thanks for the invitation, Padre," Brother said, "but when we get back from this trip I think I'm just going to sleep for about two days."

They made the final stages of the trip without serious incident, and reached their destination, a collection of little huts spread out along the riverbank and through the jungle.

"Someday," said the priest, "I want to bring them all together in one spot, in a little colony so we can take care of them better. As it is now, the supervisor can't tell who is sick and who is working."

Brother helped to unload the carts, and then after a short rest, wandered off speaking to the people. With his natural curiosity he tried to learn how they lived and how they went about gathering the rubber. That afternoon he made friends with one of the rubber workers who spoke Spanish, and early the next morning the two of them went off into the jungle on the rounds of the rubber trees. Rubber must be tapped in the morning before the heat of the day. They walked quite a distance before they encountered the first tree, and then Brother watched carefully as the Indian split the bark with a V-shaped knife, and inserted a tin cup with a spout on it.

The man turned to Brother, "Now we let it be and the rubber will run down the spout and into the cup. At noonday we shall return and empty the cup."

And so for two or three hours Brother followed the worker as he went around cutting tree after tree till finally they had marked about one hundred and fifty. They rested then and had their lunch in the quiet of the jungle, then started back to the first tree. The worker carried a rubber bag into which he emptied the contents of the cups. After the work was over, they spent a few hours hunting, returning at nightfall. In the meantime the man's wife had made a fire in a special fireplace, placing a spit above it. As Brother came up to the fire he could smell the acrid smoke and see its thick haze. The man poured the liquid rubber over the wooden crosspiece of the spit, while the woman revolved it slowly. The smoke formed a chemical reaction that coagulated the liquid. Finally, with Brother watching curiously, the liquid became a solid ball of rubber.

On his return that evening, Father Fritz asked Gonzaga how he had enjoyed his trip. Brother told him that he had found it most interesting, "In fact, Father," he said, "these people do not lead as tough a life as I thought. In the afternoon they usually get in a couple of hours of hunting."

"Nevertheless," the priest replied, "it is a monotonous life, and they are forced into a continuous search for clusters of trees. You can only tap the same tree a certain number of times. And then also they are in danger of snake bite, and they are constantly being bitten by bugs. It is the same old thing, day in and day out. About the only thing that breaks the monotony is my arrival with a load of goods. By the way, they sure snapped up all the stuff we brought. Next trip we will have to bring twice as much."

At night, stretched out on reed mats prior to sleeping, Father Fritz told Brother that they would probably leave by ten the next morning. As a matter of fact they were able to start a little earlier after the priest had said Mass for the people, and distributed communion to the few who had gone to confession the night before. They backed the oxcarts against the rubber balls, and the men inserted a long pole into the holes and lifted each one carefully onto the carts. Each ball weighed about one hundred and fifty pounds. When they had secured them tightly Father Fritz and Brother had a quick breakfast and, with a farewell to all, started on the return trip.

The load was heavy, much heavier than on the trip out, and they made slower time than Father Fritz had anticipated. The first afternoon they alternated driving the tractor and walking alongside, rearranging the rubber whenever it slipped because of the jolting of the carts. About four in the afternoon the first oxcart broke an axle and dropped into the thick yellow dust, rolling its cargo into the jungle bordering the road. In a moment everything was in chaos as the other carts began toppling over. Brother who was driving at the time stopped immediately, but the damage was done.

It meant spending the rest of the evening on the spot. First of all, one of the Indians went into the jungle to cut a new axle. When this was put in place, and the wheels once again attached to the cart, they labored to reload the rubber, sweating and groaning in the heat.

By the time they had finished the task, it was time to prepare a late supper of *charqui* and rice. The next day, as luck would have it, as they were crossing the *pampa*, (the long expanse of treeless plain) another of the oxcarts broke an axle. Father Fritz by this time was tired almost past endurance. He stretched out on the ground and rested before he even dared to issue orders. Then, his face grimy with sweat, he managed a grin at Brother. "Kill the motor, Brother," he said, "and get the guns out. We're going hunting. We have been pushing too hard. If we don't get some fresh meat soon, we are never going to make it."

They walked slowly across the plain keeping their eyes peeled for partridges among the thick clumps of grass. "I don't expect that we will get anything big," Father Fritz said, "but we ought to get a couple of birds and perhaps even a monkey."

Brother's stomach flipped over at the mention of monkey. Since he had been on the mission he had known that sooner or later he would have to eat monkey. He didn't relish the idea at all. "Someone told me on the launch that the monkeys cry like little babies when you have them cornered and are going to shoot them. Is there any truth to that?"

"I guess they were talking about the monkey we call the *manechi,*" the priest replied. "They don't really cry, but they do have a voice box and they sort of whimper. They don't have intelligence any more than other animals, of course, but I hate shooting them. As a matter of fact, I never shoot an animal unless we need food. And I never shall. But one thing is for sure, God put them here to serve and feed man, and since they can't preach the Gospel, and I can, I have no scruples over killing them to keep on going."

Just then they spied two partridges running awkwardly through the grass, and Father Fritz had his gun up and fired before Brother had his to shoulder height. They gathered the birds, left the *pampa* and went into the jungle.

"There is some pretty good hunting around here, Brother," Father Fritz told him. "We have the *joci,* a rodent about the size of a small ferret dog that has the best meat you ever tasted. Then there is the *colorado* which is a little larger, but its meat is not as good. And the *capiguara* of course, which is the largest rodent in

South America. It gets as big as a young heifer sometimes and can weigh as much as 150 pounds. It has a long tail and is a good swimmer. But the natives prefer to get a good shot at the *taititu* which is a wild pig that travels not in bands, but only with his mate. It has good meat and the people dry the hide in the sun and trade it for a couple of boxes of shells."

"What do we do if we run into a band of wild pigs?" Brother asked. "I hear that they can be dangerous and tree a man."

"Well, the best thing is to get off to one side of them if possible, but if the jungle is too thick, then climb a tree. If they attack the tree, swing to another one and then another. If they ever get you they can slash you to pieces with their tusks. I never bother with them, though, since their meat has too much muscle for good eating. Sometimes, when a herd of them comes near the village, the Indians will get behind them and pick them off one at a time."

"Once in awhile we get a small deer, called the *venado*, which is pretty tasty, and with a bit of luck, a pheasant now and then; and of course there are always doves."

"How about really wild animals?"

"You seldom see any of them. Just the damage they have done and a few carcasses they have left behind. The most common around here is the mountain lion and the black panther, although not so many of the latter."

They wandered through the jungle for almost two hours and finally ended up with the partridges and six doves. "That ought to hold us for tonight, anyway," the priest said.

When they got back to the tractor they found that the Indians had repaired the axle but had not yet reloaded the carts. "Leave it that way till morning," Father Fritz said, "and let's build a fire and have a good dinner. That's the best thing about this road, Brother; you can leave it blocked all night and feel sure that no one will come along to pass." They had a choice of roasting the birds on a spit or over a sheet of iron, but finally decided to do the birds *cacciatore*—hunter's stew. It tasted marvelous after the *charqui* and rice they had been eating, and they went to bed with the first full stomachs in a couple of days.

During the early part of the night, Father Fritz thought he heard Brother moaning softly but fell asleep again before he could check. Finally, at three in the morning, he awakened completely and saw Brother pacing back and forth across the *pampa* saying his Rosary. He lit a cigarette and went over to him.

"What's the matter, Brother? Can't sleep?"

"I got a couple of hours, Padre, but this stomach of mine is on the bum again. Must of eaten too much of that stew."

It suddenly struck Father Fritz that for the last couple of days Brother had been walking with a slight stoop, partly doubled over in fact. He must have been in pain all the time, the priest thought, and I was paying so much attention to the rubber and the tractor and my own little aches that I never noticed it. His first thought was that Brother had somehow strained himself with all the lifting, but then he remembered that Gonzaga still worked just as hard as ever with no notable strain. The pain must be an internal one, and since it was constant, it must also be a serious one. The priest was alarmed. When he spoke he left no doubt in Brother's mind that he really wanted him to get examined as soon as possible.

"You better get that checked when you get back to Riberalta. It could be amoebas, or liver trouble, or any number of things. If you let it go, you might get into real trouble."

"I'll see the Sister at the hospital when I get back," Brother promised. "It's going away now and I'm going to try to get an hour's sleep."

They found the mission running smoothly when they got back, and Brother spent the next few days cleaning the tractor. When it came time for the next trip, Father Fritz told him he would go alone. He told Brother that he ought to rest up and take care of his stomach. For the first day Gonzaga was restless and a little lonely after the priest had gone, but then he started to walk around the little pueblo and soon was learning a lot of things that would come in useful later.

There was the tanning, for example. The Indians took the hides and removed some of the hair by scraping and then employed two trees in the tanning process. Potash from one of the trees was used for softening. They filled a hollowed-out tree trunk with the solution and soaked the hides for long periods. Then the hides were taken out and scraped once, then more, then placed back in the solution for more softening.

Next to the tanning site was the brick-making section.

The Indians worked with their feet, kneading a mixture of dirt, *pampa* grass, and water till thoroughly blended. This was put into forms and allowed to dry in the sun. One of the workers described how they made the kiln itself. From bricks already dried in the sun, they fashioned an oven about the size of a small room. On the four sides little windows are left open for peepholes. In front, low down, was a small door for feeding the fuel. Over the fire an arch was made of dried mud bricks larger than the usual size, and on top of the arch three layers of the prepared brick were placed. At first only a smudge fire is lit, but gradually the fire is built up and burned furiously for about three days. Then the entire structure, including the doorway, is sealed and left to cool for a week. At the end of that time the oven is peeled apart, brick by brick, and if there was a good burning, the bricks come out ready for building.

Brother was surprised to learn that the carpenter was not a native of Cavinas but had been brought in to do some of the finer work, such as furniture and church decorations. He was a master craftsman named Elias, a small man with a mustache and a toothless grin. When Brother walked into his shop he was sawing a board in the peculiar way of South American carpenters. They reverse the saw and saw away from instead of towards themselves, as American carpenters do. He was in the process of making several chairs for the mission, and in a primitive assembly-line way had already made all the legs, and was now working on the backs. He explained to Brother that it was easier to make the same piece several times over, once you got into the swing of it, rather than completing each chair separately.

He took Brother out back and showed him how the Indians made the boards. "Father picks out the trees, then they are cut down, and dragged here with the tractor. The Indians saw them with a big cross cut."

Brother saw that they had dug a big pit, deeper than a man, and that the log was suspended over this pit on two saw horses. One man down in the pit and one man on a framework above the log wielded the saw up and down.

But the work that Elias was most proud of was the cylinders he had made for pressing the sugar cane. He showed the apparatus to Brother with a gleam in his eye and pride in his voice. He had made three wooden cylindrical gears and set them upright so that they meshed with each other. The sugar cane was fed into the first gear, and a couple of little Indian boys grabbed it as it came out and fed it into the next gear. The juice ran into troughs and finally into hollowed-out logs used as reservoirs. Later it would be converted into sugar by boiling over brick fires, and alcohol was also distilled for use in the infirmary.

Father Fritz was exhausted when he came back from the second trip and decided to let the rest of the rubber go until later. He made it back just in time to escape being caught out on the *pampa* in one of the famous *surazos*. The *surazo* is a cold spell that sets in with a biting wind blowing from the South, followed by a damp, drizzly rain. It chills to the marrow, and the Indians, who have no heating facilities, wrap themselves in all their available clothing and wait miserably for it to pass. The horses stand motionless for hours on end in the slanting rain, their backs to the winds, their tails between their legs, looking forlorn and pitiable.

Brother bundled himself up and stayed to his room writing a few letters and compiling a list of things he would need when he got back to his workshop in Riberalta. Father Fritz caught up on his mission accounts and wrote a stack of letters for Brother to mail from Riberalta. Finally, on the last morning of the *surazo*, they heard the whistle of the launch. Brother who had been packed for days, not knowing when the launch would arrive, hurried down to the port.

On arrival at the shore he discovered that the launch would stay in port for the day and leave the next morning. Brother deposited his things on board and returned to the rectory with Father Fritz. "Brother," Father Fritz said, "I haven't had a chance to show my gratitude, and I have been so busy with the rubber that I haven't been able to see that you have been eating properly. We should have a real meal tonight, since only the Good Lord knows what you will eat aboard the launch. How does your stomach feel?"

"I've taken such good care of it the last several days that the pain has gone away, and frankly, Father, I could stand a good healthy meal."

"Wonderful. What would you like in the way of meat—*joci, venado,* monkey or *colorado?* You name it and we'll get it."

"You're bragging now," Brother said. "It is one o'clock in the afternoon and you guarantee that you can have any type of animal I want by dinner time?"

Father Fritz had been extending himself a little in making the promise but he refused to back down. "Just name it," he said.

"Okay. This I will have to see. I'll take that *joci* that you have been bragging so much about."

Father Fritz turned to one of the little Indian boys and said, "Ignacio, we need a *joci* real bad. Whom shall we see?"

"I think, *padrecito,*" the Indian said, "that maybe René."

"Wait a minute," Brother said, "that doesn't count. I thought you would have to go out and kill one. If someone already has one prepared, that's a different thing."

Father Fritz smiled mysteriously, obviously enjoying himself. "I guarantee you that the *joci* is still in the jungle, that it is still alive, and that you will be eating it for dinner!" Then turning to the Indian boy, he said, "Call René, *por favor.*"

René came walking up to them in a few minutes. He was dressed in khaki trousers and shirt, and leather sandals. "I hear that you have a *joci,*" Padre Fritz said, "I need one for Brother here and I will pay well. Will you sacrifice him?"

"But of course, *padrecito,*" René said, "you will have him before sunset."

"All right," Brother said. "I give up. What's it all about?" The priest laughed. "Bro, I've been pulling your leg. The people around here know the animals so well and they can read their signs so clearly, that they watch for a certain animal to set up a pattern. After a while they know when a particular one will pass by a certain spot at the same time each day; for the animals, like ourselves, are creatures of habit. The people don't always need the food, so they just leave the animal alone till they need it. All the neighbors keep hands off because the other man saw it first. They say 'that's Ignacio's *venado*' or 'that's René's *joci.*'

"So right now René has a *joci* lined up that he was saving for an occasion."

"Well, it's hard to believe," Brother said, "but I'll take your word for it."

"Don't take my word for it," the priest rejoined, "let's go along with René and see for ourselves."

René told them that his animal passed a certain spot about four-thirty on his way for water. They left in mid-afternoon and walked through the jungle for three quarters of an hour or so till René silenced them with a backward wave of his hand and brought the little procession to a halt. He went forward silently and alone, and then came back grinning and nodding his head.

"He hasn't checked for a day or two," Father Fritz whispered to Brother, "that nod means that the animal passed here yesterday as usual."

While they watched him, René carefully loaded his gun, and then when he thought it about time, motioned for them to retreat a distance and be silent. Hiding behind a low tree he placed his gun in the crotch and pointed it at a certain spot in the underbrush. He remained that way immobile minute after minute. Brother crouched almost without breathing, and then just as he thought he would surely have to move from his cramped position, the gun went off.

There was a slight thrashing about in the brush and René went forward and shouted back. "There it is."

As Father Fritz had promised, they ate roasted *joci* that night on the back porch of the rectory and Gonzaga found it the sweetest and most tender meat he had ever tasted. Over his second helping he said, "Padre, my humblest apologies. I never thought there was such a thing as a mail order house for wild animals!"

They sat there for a time after the table had been cleared, grateful for the warmth of the night after the bone-shivering *surazo.* Father Fritz turned to Gonzaga, "Brother," he said, "I'm going to miss you. It has been nice having someone around."

"It has been good for me, too, Father. I've learned a lot and I can appreciate how easy I have it in Riberalta. Tell me, will you, how is it to live without any other priests? Don't you ever get lonely?"

The priest did not answer for a long while, mulling over the question, knowing that it was an important one, and wanting to get his answer just right.

"Yes, I suppose that I do get lonely once in awhile. These are good people and I love them, but their interests are limited. I have a lot of work here, but after a time it becomes pretty much routine. I seldom receive a new book or a magazine, and the launch comes along with a letter or two only at long intervals. Most of the time, as I say, I'm occupied, but every now and then I long for a little bit of English, to speak to someone who thinks like I do.

"I don't think I feel it as much as some of the other

fellows do, though. One of the priests was telling me he even got to the point where he hated to see a visitor. He told me that it took him about two weeks to get into the set schedule and routine of his mission, to a point where he dulled his senses just a little, living slightly under the level of full awareness. Just as he had it worked out, along would come a visitor. They would sit up all night talking about a million things, and in the morning the visitor would be gone, leaving this priest all stirred up. It would take him another two weeks to get back his calm. After doing this repeatedly, he felt it took too much out of him and he used to shudder each time he saw a friend getting off the launch.

"I'll admit that is a little extreme, but I guess everyone suffers from loneliness a little bit."

"I got a glimpse of it," Brother supplied, "while you were gone for the rubber. I felt kind of lost the first couple of days. I guess I ought to thank God that Brothers don't have to live alone."

"On the other hand," Father Fritz said, "it is sometimes a lot easier. It can be pretty difficult living with someone else. Just remember that married people don't always get along, and they have the grace of the sacrament to help them work it out. Once in a while you find yourself living in a little place like this with a fellow priest who has a personality fundamentally different from yours. No matter how much each of you try, you are bound occasionally to get on each others nerves. You don't like the way he coughs when he gets up in the morning; he doesn't like the way you push your food around on the plate between mouthfuls. Given time he doesn't even like the way you chew.

"What makes it more difficult, of course, is the fact that you can't get away from each other. You can't just walk down the street and buy yourself a meal, or go to a movie."

The priest began to chuckle. "I heard a good story about two priests in China who had it worked out pretty well. They were good friends, but they had been cooped up for a long time and they felt themselves getting tight. By mutual agreement they worked out a system. There was a large, screened-in porch just outside their respective rooms, so they agreed that neither one would enter the room of the other. But if one of them felt the need of talking or of companionship, he would go out and sit on the porch. The other one could see him, of course, and if he felt up to it would go out and talk for a time. If he had work to do, or just felt a little nasty, he stayed in his room. They tell me that they remained good friends all their lives and they attribute it to their little system."

"Of course, Brother," he added, "loneliness isn't peculiar to the missionary life. There are hundreds of thousands of people sitting in lonely rooms in the States, and they haven't even got the good fortune of having the motive that we have."

"Don't I know it?" Brother answered. "Many a lonely night I spent on the road in the old days. Well, if it is okay by you, I better get some sleep. That launch leaves early in the morning."

"Good," Father Fritz said, "I'll get you up in time and see you off."

CHAPTER 13

Bishop Danehy who as Father Danehy had made that first trip from Cochabamba to Riberalta with Brother and who had replaced Bishop Escalante when the latter went to Mexico on a special assignment, frequently made the trip to Cavinas with Brother Gonzaga. It was part of his job as Superior of the mission to visit the outposts, but in addition, he liked to get away from the desk work in Riberalta and the daily routine.

Out on the river with Brother, Bishop Danehy could relax in old clothes and feel that thrill of navigating the old *Innisfail* through a ticklish spot or two. On one particular trip in early 1949, the two of them made a fast run to Cavinas with just the cook on board. Bishop Danehy, thin and lean, was dressed in old khaki trousers and a ragged shirt, looking like a beachcombing Gregory Peck. Brother, as usual, was fussing with the motor, his face smudged with diesel oil. The bishop turned the wheel over to the cook for a spell and went back to where Brother was working.

"Bro," he said, "what do you say if we knock off for a while and get a swim before we tie up for the night?"

"Okay, Bishop," Brother said. "Give me a couple of

more minutes on this thing and we can pull in anytime."

The bishop smiled inwardly to himself as he watched Brother finish up the job. Gonzaga looked up and caught the bishop grinning at him. "What's so funny?" he asked.

"I was just thinking, Brother," the bishop said, "what my friends back in the States would say if they could see me dressed like this."

"Well, I guess it would strike them as kind of funny," Brother replied. "But one thing is for sure, those khakis are a lot cooler than Bishop's robes, and if you fall overboard, you'll find the swimming a lot easier."

"I'm not complaining, Brother," the bishop laughed. "It just struck me as funny. I rather enjoy it. Come on, finish that up and let's get that dip."

They had their swim and Gonzaga took the wheel while the bishop sat watching the play of the sunset on the river. Brother turned halfway around to face the bishop, "I hope you brought along enough insulin this time," he said.

"You worry about it more than I do. Of course, I've got enough insulin. Stop worrying."

"Can't help it," Brother answered. "What if we have motor trouble and get stuck up here?"

"I'll just stop eating and float down river in a canoe. Sometimes you make me feel like an old grandmother, always checking on the insulin and making sure I've got a tin of hard candy on board. Nowadays, Brother, diabetics live longer than other people. Someone is always taking care of them."

"Okay, it's your funeral," Gonzaga said. But he didn't feel that way about it. He knew that it took a pretty special kind of courage to live with diabetes in a place where every drop of insulin had to be flown in. He had to hand it to the bishop all right.

For his own part, staring off into the gathering darkness, the bishop was thinking that it took a special kind of virtue for Brother Gonzaga to keep going like this without the consolation of administering the sacraments and with little chance to preach the Word. "He has to do it all by good example," the bishop thought.

As if they could sense what the other was thinking, Brother turned around just in time to smile happily back at the bishop. They looked at each other for a second, feeling that camaraderie that men sometimes feel, then Gonzaga turned back to the wheel. "It's always kind of peaceful out here, this time of night," he said shyly.

They stopped that night at a small pueblo and the bishop held night prayers and talked to the people. Brother noticed that a man gave the bishop a message after night prayers, but he was busy with something else and didn't pay much attention. He saw Bishop Danehy read it by the light of one of the candles, and after thanking the man, fold the paper and put it in his cassock pocket.

He was a little surprised when the bishop decided to sleep on board the launch as Brother himself invariably did. "I think I'll keep you company tonight," was all the bishop said by way of explanation.

They arranged the mosquito netting satisfactorily on board, and bedded down for the night, but it was a long time before the bishop fell asleep. Brother could hear him moving around restlessly on his cot. He, himself fell asleep shortly afterwards, only to be awakened by the light patter of rain on the roof. He dashed outside to cover up the engine well and found the bishop there first. By the time they had things shipshape they were both soaked to the skin. After they had dried themselves they sat there listening to the storm, feeling the launch sway with the gusts of wind. Their cigarettes tasted moldy and they dragged as though they had been soaked in water, but it felt good to be inside out of the storm.

Like all tropical storms this one blew itself out quickly. Brother arose to go back to his cot but the bishop stopped him. "Brother," he said, "I've been trying to tell you something. They gave me a message back there." He hesitated, then said quickly, "It came from Riberalta, and it said they had received news that your mother had died. I know how you feel and I guess you'd like to be left alone. I'll say Mass for her soul in the morning." The bishop couldn't look at him as Brother made his way to the forward cabin.

Just before dawn, he saw Gonzaga sitting on the hatch over the motor. It had become his favorite position on all his trips. "How is it going, Brother?" he asked quietly.

Gonzaga looked up and smiled slowly. "It's okay, Bishop. It's as we tell the people. It isn't any good to go on about it. She was a saint and I've been praying my rosary for her. I'm sure she is up there with the Blessed Mother. With your Mass now, I'll be more sure of it. And thanks a lot, Bishop, for being so nice about it."

When Brother returned to Riberalta he found a letter

from his old friend Bishop Lane. This is what he wrote in reply:

My heartfelt thanks for your kindness. When word came that God had called my Mom home, I was on the river with Bishop Danehy on the way to Cavinas. I like to think that she would be wanting me to be doing just that. I feel so much closer to her now, and she has helped me much already. I am sure she will be eternally grateful to you for your prayers.

There is a lot of noise tonight as we are in carnival time, a week of fiesta. None of these people seem to know what it is all about, what it means, or how it started, but they do, in their own way, have a great devotion for the Passion of Our Lord, and the way of the Cross is always well attended in Lent.

We had quite a trip to Cavinas. It took six days to reach there, and it rained most of the time and our cots and bedding were kind of damp when we stretched out at night. The people along the river are always very kind. They have so little but they are always willing to share it. One night we stopped at a *choco* where there were but about two houses, and the good man started to complain of the government not doing anything for the Beni. He wanted to know why they didn't build a railroad from La Paz to Riberalta and run it through his place. Another place a man was pretty well set up with pigs and chickens and even a milk cow, but he had no money for no one stopped there, and he expressed a great desire for a spool of thread, and a little sugar. Mass was said one morning in a chicken coop with half the roof missing. What took six days to reach, we did in twenty-eight hours coming down, the current was that strong.

All here seems to be fine, blessed by God in many ways.

We hope we are proving grateful. Please pray for me. I do remember you every day.

In Jesus and Mary, Brother Gonzaga.

A short time later he received a letter from his brother Ernie telling about his mother's death and the funeral. He sat down at the cluttered desk in his workshop and wrote to Ernie with whom he had shared so many hardships in the early days.

You will never know how much consolation your letter gave me. I have read and reread it over and over. Yes, Ernie, Mom was a very saintly one and very close to God. I want to thank you especially for the night you spent in vigil for me. I will return that in vigils spent here in work and prayer. The thoughts that come to one's mind at a time like this are hard to put in writing. The example Mom leaves is, for us all, an open book. To serve God better that we may one day be reunited, not for a time, but for eternity. Your letter gave me a lot of hope and a heart full of joy at your resolutions. I am sure Mom smiles from heaven as she does in the picture over my desk, on all that is going on in our hearts. May Mom watch over us always and draw us ever closer to God. My best to Joe, Jennie and Lena. I pray for Lucille with all my heart. God love you, Ernie. Write to me once in awhile.

Love to all in Jesus and Mary—Charlie. Brother Gonzaga.

Not long after his Mother's death, Brother had the consolation of seeing a companion Brother arrive in the Beni. Brother Anthony from the corn country of Indiana was tall and well built, with a freckled face and a shock of blond hair. He took over some of the procurator's work and helped Brother Gonzaga with the altar boys. It was a relief to Gonzaga not to have to drop one job for another every time an emergency arose. Brother Anthony moved right in and became Gonzaga's right arm. Most important, of course, was the chance to lead a little of community life with another Brother. Not that Gonzaga had not been happy living more or less alone as a Brother, but sometimes it can be a great help to sit down and talk to someone who speaks the same language about tools and machines.

Despite the lessening of the burden of work, Gonzaga began more and more to feel the stomach pains that had bothered him in Cavinas. He tried to hide his acute discomfort but inevitably it was called to the attention of Bishop Danehy. Finally in May of 1951 Brother was sent to the hospital at Lima for a complete checkup. In his own words, Gonzaga tells about his illness in a letter to the bishop. "How are you? I just got out of the hospital. The x-rays showed that I have an ulcer, so they kept me here for awhile. The doctor said he would write Sister Mercy. He told me to take it easy for a few weeks, so I am headed for Cochabamba. Don't worry about me. What I probably need is a good big plate of spaghetti. I'll be okay."

Later he wrote, "Arrived in Cochabamba, day before yesterday. The couple of days spent here have done me a lot of good and I feel much better. I hope it will be okay with you if I spend a little more time here, then I'll be as good as ever. The pain is nearly all gone. I hope this finds you well. If there is anything I can do while here just drop me a line."

Shortly after June 8th, he wrote again, "Heard all

about your trip; I knew you were busy. Sister Mercy gave me the news and told me all about the weeping at her going. She was crying when she was retelling the story. I have been kind of anxious to get back but Sister told me I should stay a few more weeks. In the past week I have felt fine, and put on a couple of pounds, so I hope to come back full of zip."

Without ever once complaining yet knowing that he was going back to ill-prepared food and all the things that complicate ulcers, Brother was back in Riberalta in July, and off on one trip by August and then on another with the bishop and Father Tom Collins up the Beni river. That Christmas he had Brother Anthony to help with the festivities which he describes in a letter to Bishop Lane:

> We had a wonderful Christmas. Our crib was built in the form of a *golpon.* It is the type of house the jungle rubber-worker lives in with just four poles and a thatched roof. The little tykes stared wide-eyed at the Child in the straw, wondering why God was born in such conditions. They stayed at the Crib so long that I wondered if the little *Niño* was talking to them, too. For the Christmas party we decorated our *golpon* with balloons. Each of the youngsters received cake, candy and a small toy. Whistles and water pistols added to the general bedlam, but noise is a small price to pay for a smiling face on a poor ragged tyke.

Before the New Year he was on a plane to Cobija where Father John Fowler had been pleading for someone to fix his jeep. When it came to tools Brother trusted very few people, so when he stepped off the plane he had his heavy kit in his hand. He carried it into the rectory, and the first words he asked Father Fowler were, "Where's the jeep?"

They went around the back of the house and took a look at the sorry vehicle. Brother groaned when he saw it. "Father," he said, "they ought to give priests a course in the seminary on the care of machines. How could anything ever get into this shape?" He made a detailed inspection, and then he summed it up for the priest: complete ring job, new fan belt, clean carburetor, new filter, new back spring, change of brake bands, etc., etc., etc., . . . In addition there was some plumbing work to do about the mission.

"Padre," he told Father Fowler, "if I can get a letter off to Father Gallagher in Riberalta, he can ship me up some of the things I need. If I write right now it will catch the same plane I came in on."

He wrote hurriedly, "*Muchos saludos.* Would you get Panduro to send me my pipe vise that is outside in our shed; my dies for threading half- and three-quarter inch pipe. In the storeroom he will find a fitting for connecting two turriles (metal barrels). He knows it is in a box for pipe fittings. Also I found a piece broke on the jeep, a small tube that goes to the brakes like this (here he drew an illustration), the same that we borrowed from the *municipalidad.* I have several new ones in a box in my room where jeep parts are kept. Also a new tire. I think we have two and can spare one. Please try to get these up on the next plane. Gonzaga."

On the third day of his stay, Brother came into lunch walking stiff as a ramrod and slowly eased himself into the chair across from the priest.

"What happened to you?" Father Fowler asked.

"Some joker once upon a time tried to take the wheel lugs off by turning them in the wrong direction. Now they are frozen tight. On my first attempt the spanner slipped and I thought I broke my back."

"How are you going to get them off?"

"I'm using a cold chisel and a hammer. It took me all morning just to cut through one."

They ate for awhile in silence and then Brother spoke again, "You know, Father, it's kind of crazy when you think of it. Here we are in the middle of the jungle, about as far from civilization as you can get, and we insist on complicating our lives with a lot of machinery that can only be kept up where you have good roads and plenty of spare parts. Even jeeps, which were originally invented to be expendible. You leave them out in the open for awhile and the next thing you know they are rusted solid. We put in modern plumbing with a gas pump for water, and the pump goes on the blink or the gas doesn't arrive and blooey, no water. We'd be better off going back to the oxcart like the people around here.

"In fact," and he began to laugh, "just a short time ago, I spent half a day pulling one of the Riberalta jeeps out of the mud with an oxcart."

"Maybe you're right, Brother," Father Fowler said, "and that goes for a lot of other things. We sleep in heavy beds and the mattresses become homes for insects; the people here use a nice cool hammock. We wear hot shoes and socks and the natives wear simple, airy sandals. Just to mention a few of the things. But there is a lot to be said for both sides I guess. The missioner is supposed to adapt to the life of the people and we do that in about ninety percent of the things. But on the other hand, it is a civilized world, and while some of the things we do seem nonsensical on the surface, they do have some value. Like the famous saying that an Englishman in the colonies always dresses for dinner. Some of the things we do may not be too practical in one sense, but in another way they are really necessary. They keep up our morale. They keep us going. You know, Bro, it is awful easy to let yourself go in one of these places."

Brother smiled. "You're right, Padre. Of course you're right. And I realize it. It's just that every once in awhile after working all morning on a jeep, and breaking a few tools which are irreplaceable, I lean a bit toward the other side. So," he continued, "if you will excuse me I shall now go out and keep the wheels of civilization spinning."

Shortly after Gonzaga returned to Riberalta, Brother Camillus Hoeschel arrived. And so they were three. It was getting to be quite a community. Brother Gonzaga took advantage of the extra help that Brother Camillus offered with the altar boys and the shipping, and took off for Guayaramerim to do some electrical and plumbing work for Father Gallagher, who had been transferred to that mission.

After all the manual work Gonzaga was glad to be back at Riberalta and to have the opportunity to do some spiritual work. On his first Thursday after his return he started out in the jeep with Sister Ann Elizabeth and Sister Magdalen Mary to teach catechism to youngsters out in the *campo*. The road was slippery and muddy, and at one point the jeep scooted off the road into a shallow ditch alongside. The Sisters hung on tightly and Brother gunned the motor to keep the jeep from bogging down. He could see a hornet's nest up ahead but he couldn't take a chance on stopping.

"Cover your faces!" he shouted to the Sisters and went skidding and zig-zagging up the ditch. For a minute it looked as though he might miss the nest, and then the canvas top of the jeep hit it squarely and Brother was covered with hornets. By the time they had run the length of the ditch and slithered back on the road, he was pretty badly bitten. The Sisters wanted to go back and treat him at the dispensary but Brother wouldn't hear of it. "The kids are waiting for us," he told them.

And the youngsters *were* waiting. Brother took all the boys to the nearby lake. The Sisters each took a class of girls. Sister Elizabeth Ann finished first and went looking for Brother and the jeep. She found Brother seated in the middle of a ring of youngsters, all little lads. She stood quietly on the edge of the jungle listening to the lesson Brother was teaching.

Sitting there in the midst of them with his face all swollen from the hornet bites, Brother was talking softly, "*De veras,* in truth, God is in Heaven. But He is also all around you. He is here in the clearing and there in the jungle. He sees us and hears us all the time. He is listening to me now. You see this blade of grass. He made that. He made the puppy you are holding. He made the air and the river and the fish. And the animals in the jungle. He is all around us and inside us. He lives inside you and me."

He saw Sister Ann then coming toward him. "Just finishing up, Sister," he said and then to the small fry, "Okay, beat it home now, and remember that God is watching you."

"I wish I could explain things as well as that," Sister said admiringly.

"Sister," Brother replied, "it doesn't do any good to tell these youngsters they have to go to Mass every Sunday lest they commit a mortal sin. They don't have a Sunday Mass. Or to go to the sacraments frequently, because they seldom have a chance. You have to show them God in the things they have around them every day."

Just then Sister Magdalen Mary began blowing the horn on the jeep and the two of them hurried toward her. "I don't like to hurry you, Brother, but I'd like to get back. I'm worried about Symforiana. She left us again last night."

Symforiana was mentally ill and lived for the most part on the streets. She would curl up to sleep under the seats in church, or sleep on the street outside the rectory or convent. The Sisters had a little house for the chronically sick poor, and they took her in there. But she would go off for days at a time. When apprehended she would let loose a barrage of profanity calculated to wither the ears of a monkey. Only Brother could usually bring her back without trouble.

Gonzaga left the Sisters at the Convent and after putting the jeep away, went looking for Symforiana. He looked for her in the usual places, in the church and around the hospital. Finally someone told him they had seen her going down toward the river.

He found her there standing waist deep in the water, like an animal at bay, snarling and cursing at a group of little children who were taunting her.

"*La loca, la loca, la loca,*" they were shouting in unison. The crazy one, they were calling her in a childish chant. When they saw Brother they fell silent and made room for him. He stood at the water's edge smiling at the forlorn creature in the baggy dress, at the disheveled hair and the tortured face.

"Symforiana," he said softly, "it's your friend, *hermanito*. Come on out, Symforiana." She looked suspiciously at the children and then back at Brother. Whether it was the sound of her own name, or the tone of his voice, or whether she really recognized him as her friend, he could not tell. But slowly, cautiously, still fearful of the children, she came out of the water toward him. He took her gently by the arm and led her up the bank and down the street to the Sisters' house.

He was met by the two nuns. "Sisters," he said, "I think she is pretty sick. She is trembling all over and has a terrible fever." She went quietly with all three of them to the hospital.

As Brother went quickly down the street, Sister Magdalen Mary said to her companion, "He gets so much consolation helping the sick and teaching catechism. It must be such a relief for him to get away from those motors for awhile."

Bishop Danehy, from where he was seated at his desk,

could see Brother coming down the street and he was thinking much the same thing. He was also thinking that Gonzaga was doing entirely too much of both types of work. While he never heard Brother complain, he had been watching him eat and had seen the drawn look on his face, and had concluded that it was time that Brother began slowing up. When Gonzaga came abreast of the office door he called him in.

"Brother," he began, "I don't like the way you are looking lately and I think you ought to cut down on things. I suggest that you let the other two brothers handle that long trip to teach catechism. And the altar boys take a lot out of you too. I think you ought to give them up for a while."

The expression on Brother's face was pitiable. "Bishop," he started to say, and then stopped. "Bishop," he continued after a minute, his eyes moist almost to the point of tears, "Don't take that away from me. It is the only spiritual work I have all day. The rest of it is grease and dirt, and motors. Please let me keep the altar boys. I know I can do it."

Bishop Danehy had quite a store of arguments against just such an appeal, since his own men had pointed out to him on so many occasions that he himself should slow down and take care of his diabetes. As he reviewed all the arguments in his mind, he finally concluded that none of them had much value. You might just as well burn out as rust out, he thought, and then to Gonzaga, "Okay, Brother, you can try it, but if you get seriously sick again, that's the end. At any rate, it is time for your vacation. Go on up to Cochabamba and drink in some of that mountain air."

Two days later while he was packing for his trip, Brother received a message from the hospital. He was met at the door by Sister Magdalen Mary. "Symforiana is dying of pneumonia, Brother," the nun said, "but she had one of her rare lucid moments and has received the Last Sacraments. I thought you would like to know."

Gonzaga tiptoed into the hospital room and stood beside the bed, looking down at the heavily breathing girl. It could have been that, for the first time he saw her washed up and her hair combed, or it could have been a true inner peace shining through, but he thought that she was a truly beautiful woman. She opened her eyes slowly and gradually focused on him. He reached out and took her hot hand in his. She squeezed it feebly, smiled faintly, and then closed her eyes. He saw the life go out of her.

"She was only waiting for you," the Sister said softly.

CHAPTER 14

Brother Gonzaga awakened with a start. For a second he could not remember where he was, and then it came to him. He was in bed in the Cochabamba house which the Maryknollers used for their vacations and retreats. He lay there for a moment, staring up at the ceiling, wondering what it was that had awakened him, and then suddenly it came again:

"Rat-ta-tat . . . rat-ta-tat-tat-tat—tat-tat . . . rat-rat . . . rat-tat . . ."

It certainly sounded like a machine gun, but he couldn't imagine how a machine gun could be firing behind the house at eight o'clock in the morning. His reverie was shattered by the same sound, and this time he was sure. It *was* a machine gun. There was no doubt about it.

He dressed hurriedly and dashed outside to the patio to find that Brother Alexis and the priest in charge of the house had both preceded him outdoors.

"Did I hear a machine gun?" he asked them.

"You sure did," Alexis told him, "and whoever he is, he is right up there on the hill firing over our heads."

At that moment there was the low-moaned sound of a high caliber bullet as it went singing down the lower road. And then another, and another. "Wow," Gonzaga said, "this is beginning to sound like a real, live revolution!"

"I'm afraid it is," said the priest, "and if we have any sense at all we will lock the bottom gate and stay in for a couple of days. Thank heaven we have enough food in the house."

It suddenly occurred to Brother Alexis that he and Gonzaga had seen the actual beginning of the fight. That morning they had taken a taxi to the airport at five-thirty with the idea of going to Riberalta. On arrival at the airport they had been surprised to see the plane already roaring down the field. The manager of the airport had been non-committal. "Phone later," he had said, "and we will have more information." By luck they had gotten the same taxi back to the house and gone to bed.

"Brother," Alexis said, "that pilot is probably in Argentina by now. He knew the revolution was coming off and he took the plane to keep it out of the hands of the revolutionists."

"Let's turn on the radio and see what is happening," Gonzaga said, running for the recreation room.

They waited for a few moments before they heard the announcer come on and in a breathless voice shout: "*Viva la revolucion!* The forces of the revolution in a surprise attack this morning have taken control of the two Cochabamba radio stations as well as the airport and military installations in the valley. Revolutionary forces in Santa Cruz, La Paz, and other principal places of our beloved country are routing the government forces. *Viva la revolucion!*" They waited for a few minutes and the announcer, breathless as before, repeated the same message.

"See if you can get La Paz," Alexis said to Gonzaga, who began twisting the dial. After some time he picked up music and held it, waiting for an announcement. In the middle of a very sad song of unrequited love, the announcer broke in. "In a surprise attack this morning, the revolutionary forces attempted to take control of Cochabamba, Santa Cruz and La Paz. Government forces have the situation in hand and have routed the rebels. Citizens remain in your homes! *Viva el gobierno!*"

"Well," Gonzaga said, "that's par for the course. The battle has just begun and both sides have already won it." They spent the rest of the day alternately hearing the government and revolutionist claiming victory, all the while hoping that the machine gunner on the hill would not get bored and lower his sights on their house. In late afternoon someone appeared to have silenced the machine gun, or what is more probable the gunner just ran out of ammunition. Anyway the machine gun was silent, and except for the occasional *ping* of a bullet down on the road, things were quiet.

The two Brothers had left all their baggage in the airline office the afternoon before, and now they began to think about a change of underclothing. Every religious common house in the world has a bag of assorted odds and ends that were returned from the laundry only after their owners, visiting members of the community, had long since moved on. It was to this treasure-trove that the two of them went hunting. Brother Alexis, who was well over six feet and built in proportion, found nothing that would fit. Gonzaga, who was more average in build, made out pretty well. "That's the trouble with you big fellows," he told Alexis, "comes the revolution and you're more trouble than you're worth."

After dinner that night, the two of them sat in the recreation room playing a game of two-handed rummy. Gonzaga, who enjoyed playing cards, was losing as usual when suddenly there was a knock on the door. Since the door led to a darkened patio, and was at least half a mile from the road where there was still occasional shooting, they were both startled. The first thought that came to both of them was that either the government or the revolutionary forces had finally arrived on the scene.

Brother Gonzaga got up slowly and walked toward the door. Before opening it he turned to Alexis and said, "Say a prayer, Brother, that they don't start shooting." He opened the door quickly, expecting to find soldiers with leveled guns. He moved backward in surprise when he saw that the visitors were a couple of Indians. The man spoke first. "*Padrecito,*" he pleaded, "my baby is sick and we want him baptized." Brother still a bit dazed and very, very thankful, found the priest in charge saying his breviary in the chapel, and assisted at the baptism. When Gonzaga came back he was still a little shaky.

"All I could think of," he said, "was what I had read in detective stories. Never stand with the light behind you. And there I was with the lamp shining on me and them in darkness."

"While you were gone," Alexis said, "I was thinking how convenient a revolution could be to a couple of fellows who didn't like each other. The revolution begins, so you go next door and knock off the lad you don't like. When the revolt is over he is found, and everyone chalks it up to a stray bullet. I'll bet a lot of fellows make out pretty well in a revolution like this."

"You couldn't be more right," Gonzaga said. "The last revolution in Riberalta, there was a fellow in town who hated the *commandante.* The day the revolt started he walked into the office of the commander and showered him with bullets. Never gave him a chance. The revolutionists lost and the murderer escaped into Brazil. A couple of months later an amnesty was declared and he was back in Riberalta, and everything was forgotten."

On the morning of the third day of the revolt the government-controlled radio in La Paz broadcast a message from the President. Government troops were marching on Cochabamba, which was in the hands of the revolutionists, and if the city did not surrender by nightfall, government planes would begin a systematic bombing of the valley the next day.

The revolutionists who had a fairly accurate idea of the bombing potential of the government forces, refused to surrender. The next morning Gonzaga and Alexis sat on the front lawn waiting for the government planes. About eleven in the morning, they heard the drone of motors off in the distance. Two antiquated DC 3's hove into sight. They lumbered right over the Maryknoll house at a low altitude and circled the city. As they came back, the Brothers could see something drop out of the planes. Then they heard a slight explosion. The planes repeated the maneuver and left through the mountain pass in the direction of the capital. "They must be dropping firecrackers," Gonzaga said. Later on they found out his guess wasn't far from wrong. The crews of the DC's had dumped several dynamite-filled artillery shells out the plane's rear door. The bombs had killed one cow and started a small fire in a gasoline dump at the airport.

The revolution lasted two weeks and the government finally won out. But it was a full month before the airline began operations again, when the scattered planes had been brought back from their refuge in other countries. Brother Alexis had long since returned to Peru overland as Gonzaga prepared to leave for Riberalta.

Once on the plane, the pilot invited Brother up to sit in the cockpit. He was the same pilot, Brother discovered, who had taken off so hurriedly the morning he and Alexis had gone to the airport. "Someone tipped me off," the pilot told him, "and I figured I had better get out of there before I got myself shot and my plane stolen. So I headed for Argentina and waited it out.

"The whole thing didn't amount to much, I guess, but I heard a funny story about the fighting in Cochabamba. It seems that the revolutionists were in the plaza firing at the police who were up on the roof of the prefecture. The Indians were standing at all the street entrances to the square, watching the proceedings. Why no one was killed by a stray bullet. I'll never know. Anyway the

Indians thought it was better than a fiesta. Suddenly in the midst of the firing an ice cream vendor forced his way through the crowd and started to walk around the plaza pushing his cart. He kept shouting *helados* (ice cream) every couple of feet. The Indians began to laugh and the next thing you know the firing stopped on both sides while he made the complete round of the plaza. All you could hear was this lad's shouting *helados* and the laughing of the Indians."

Brother told him about the Indian who had come for the baptism and they all had a good laugh. When Brother went back to his seat he said his rosary for the souls of those who had been killed, reflecting all the while on the simplicity of these people who looked on death with such little concern.

Although Gonzaga did not know it, time was running out for himself. In a few short months he would be dead. In the meantime he celebrated his fifteenth anniversary in Maryknoll on October 17th, and in answer to a letter from Bishop Lane he wrote:

> Many thanks for the anniversary remembrance and for your prayers. We just finished our retreat, and the Fathers are now being scattered to the four winds. It looks like Grand Central Station, except that they are leaving mostly in canoes. We celebrated the Feast of Christ the King with a big bang. A solemn Mass and a procession of the Blessed Sacrament through the main plaza. *Viva Christo Rey* (Long live Christ the King!) was shouted all over the place. It must have been somewhat like the procession of Our Lord on Palm Sunday, with little kids running all over coming to look at Our Lord in the Sacred Host, throwing flowers

and with lots of noise. But when one gets to understand these people, one realizes that to Our Lord it is all a prayer and their simple way of showing homage. At the time when Our Lord is raised in benediction there is a great silence, and I could not help but notice the contrast. So with God's blessing they resume their hard life, somewhat happier and their burden lighter. Everyone here seems to be in good health and raring to go. We have been blessed in many ways, and we hope we are proving grateful by being faithful. Many thanks again and *muchos saludos* from Maryknoll south of the border. Pray for me and be assured of my daily prayers.

On November 21, 1951, the Feast of the Presentation of Our Lady, Brother was in the chapel at Riberalta saying the Little Office. Beside him on the bench, dozing quietly, was Alegria, a small mongrel dog that had taken to Brother and followed him wherever he went. In the choir loft, one of the Sisters was practicing with the choir girls.

For several days Brother had not been feeling well, and now with the singing above him and the pain inside him, he was finding it difficult to concentrate on the words of the Office. Suddenly he felt an agonizing pain and cried out softly, dropping his book and bending over double in the pew. He struggled to his feet and still bent over, sweat pouring out of him and pain like an iron claw in his stomach, he inched his way out the door to his combination workshop and bedroom. Alegria, sensing something wrong, thumped her tail once or twice on the bench and with a low whine followed him. The Sister who had her back turned to the body of the Church saw nothing.

Once in his room Gonzaga eased himself down on the bed, crying softly with the pain and reciting ejaculations over and over. When it became worse, he got out of bed and knelt at its foot, holding on to the iron frame with a grip that almost twisted the metal. When the bleeding started, the pain went away, and he slumped exhausted to the floor.

It was here that Bishop Danehy found Gonzaga some time later and had him taken to the hospital. When they had bedded him down, Brother asked the Bishop to give him the Last Sacraments. "Bishop," he whispered, "I think this is it. The bleeding won't stop." Bishop Danehy heard his confession and gave him Extreme Unction. Brother passed the night restlessly.

During the night they checked the bleeding and fed him glucose, and in the morning when Sister Francis Jerome came in to check on him, he was awake and feeling a little better. He smiled weakly and said, "I thought I was going to die last night, Sister. I was so happy because I always wanted to die on our Lady's feast. I have prayed for that favor."

A short time later Bishop Danehy came in to see him. "Brother," he told him, "as soon as you get well enough, you're going stateside. It is almost time for your leave anyway."

Brother grimaced, this time not with the pain, but at the thought of going back to the States. "I don't want to go back, Bishop," he said, "you know what will happen. They'll keep me there with this ulcer."

"Well, they have to think of you, Brother. Maybe

with good treatment and a good diet, the thing will clear up and you can get a clean bill of health. Anyway don't think about it for now, and we'll talk to Bishop Lane when he comes for his visitation."

After the Bishop had gone, Gonzaga lay there thinking. He had no more ties in the States. It would be nice to say hello to Ernie and his sister, but Mom was dead, and he had no friends left there. Down here was his life. He had made it his home.

His thoughts were interrupted by Sister Ruth Patrice tiptoeing into the room. "I know how devoted you are to the Little Flower," she said, "and I brought you a crucifix of mine that contains one of her relics."

"Thank you, Sister," he said, "I am very grateful. I'll give it back to you when I am better."

And better he did become. Bit by bit, with just diet and good care on the part of the Sisters, the ulcer was controlled. He was released from the hospital on another feast of the Blessed Mother, her Immaculate Conception.

Before he left the hospital he gave the crucifix back to Sister Ruth Patrice. She has never forgotten what he said to her. "Sister," he told her, "always keep this crucifix. It will carry you through all trials."

He was well enough and feeling like his old self by Christmas time. He gave a big party for the altar boys. Bishop Danehy and all the priests attended the party out of respect for Brother and to show how glad they were at his recovery. He took a lot of kidding, as usual, but deep inside he felt mixed emotions. The dreaded decision on whether or not he would go back to the States was coming closer and closer. Bishop Lane was already in South America, headed for the Beni.

In late January of 1952 Bishop Lane arrived in Riberalta.

CHAPTER 15

Bishop Lane took Brother Gonzaga for a stroll around the plaza the first evening he was in Riberalta. "Brother," he said, "I have been told that you have been very sick. We are thinking of moving your leave up a couple of months."

Brother Gonzaga looked off toward the river, pretending not to hear. "Bishop," he said, "I'm afraid that the *Innisfail* isn't in shape for your trip to Cavinas. I think we ought to hire another launch, just to be on the safe side."

The Bishop laughed. "Don't try to pull that on me, Brother," he said. "You heard me well enough. When we come back down river, you better start packing."

"Will you let me come back?" Gonzaga begged him.

"I can't guarantee a thing, Brother, and you know it. I have a council and they have something to say. But if that ulcer clears up in the States, we'll certainly do what we can to send you back here. What were you saying about the *Innisfail?*"

"I said it wasn't in too good shape and while I would use it myself, I don't think you ought to take a chance, what with being Superior General."

"Well, if you are worrying about me dying, you can

forget it. In the first place I'm getting to be an old man and it would be kind of nice to finish up on the missions. And if you are worrying about the expense of electing a new Superior General, you can forget that too. My council took out enough insurance on my life to finance a whole new Chapter. What's wrong with the launch anyway?"

"Oh, just the same old trouble with the pump. I always manage to get it fixed, somehow, but you can be sure it will fail several times on the trip up river."

"Well, we'll take a chance on it then, Brother. I promised myself, the last time I was here, that I would take a trip on that launch if it is the last thing I do. And by heavens we'll make it this time. I won't be down this way again, you know."

"Alright, Bishop," Brother gave in, "by the time you come back from Guayaramerim I ought to have it in pretty good order. I hope."

Gonzaga spent the next several days working on the launch. When he had the motor in as good shape as it ever was, he cleaned the deck and the cabins. As a finishing touch he hung some holy pictures in the cabins. In the front cabin he placed a picture of the Little Flower over the tiller. When Bishop Lane came aboard with Father Raymond Bonner, all set for the trip, this picture was the first thing that they noticed. Brother saw their glances. "This trip is under her protection," he told them firmly, as though expecting opposition. They both thought it a good idea, and said so.

All the Sisters and the priest who were stationed in Riberalta came down to see them off. At the last minute

Brother excused himself, clambered up the steep bank to one of the Sisters and asked her to put a vigil light in front of the statue of the Blessed Virgin and to keep it lit all the time they were gone for the success of the trip. He returned to the boat with a light heart, feeling that he had done all in his power to make it a good trip, now that it was under the protection of his two patronesses.

The first day out Bishop Lane took the wheel and Brother hovered over the motor like the proverbial mother hen. There were six of them on board the first day. The Superior General, Bishop Lane; the Prefect Apostolic of the Beni, Bishop Danehy; The Society Superior of South America, Father Bonner; Father Thomas Higgins and Brother Gonzaga; and lastly, Ignacio, the cook.

While Bishop Lane piloted, Brother tended the motor, and Ignacio readied the meals, the others sat around writing letters, saying their breviaries or checking on the equipment. It was crowded on deck and in the two small cabins, and occasionally they would clamber up on the roofs and just talk, or sit there feeling the hot sun. They spent the first night at a small settlement called Candalaria, and as they were tying up Brother took the occasion to tell Bishop Lane what a good job he had done of navigating a particularly tricky spot in the river. The Bishop was as pleased as a bride over her first roast.

They dropped Father Higgins off at Candalaria and took aboard Father Felix McGowan and a young boy he had along with him, and began the second day of the trip. It turned out to be a long and tedious one for Brother. They had several breakdowns, but each time, sweating and working like a demon, he managed to get the motor started again.

They spent the night at San Miguel and went on the third day. Halfway through the afternoon, with the motor running well for a change, Brother washed up and came to the front cabin where Father Bonner was piloting.

They talked about the river and the trip and many things in general. Finally the talk got around to the parish in Riberalta. "You know, Father," Brother said, "if I were a priest I wouldn't talk so much about going to Mass and receiving the sacraments. I think I would talk about calumny. So many times these people murder each other with their tongues. It seems to be a national pastime. It makes it difficult for anyone to have confidence in the other person."

"There is sure an awful lot of it," the priest said, "I guess that communities, and perhaps even nations have some particular defect just like individuals. But just clearing up that defect isn't always the answer. There isn't any one solution to any problem it seems to me. You have to attack the whole gamut of things . . . the big defect and the little ones.

"And the priest in a parish has to think of developing the whole life of his people. That's why he just can't preach any one thing to the exclusion of everything else. Even in our own spiritual lives," he continued, "we may have one particular devotion or prayer that helps us tremendously, but we don't neglect the rest of our religious exercises."

"That's true, Padre," Brother said, "ever since I heard a priest preach on the acts of faith, hope and charity, and how if you keep making them constantly you gradually grow in their virtues. I have been making that my principal devotion. But on the other hand I have my Little Office that I say and my special prayers to the Blessed Mother and to the Little Flower, and my Holy Hour."

"A lot of people," Father Bonner said, "think that for any given problem there is usually a single, simple solution. Even missioners, who should know better, sometimes fall victim to this. A priest will come along and see a certain need and his solution to it is to build schools. Let everything else go hang. Or another one will come along and he gets the idea that everything will be solved if we just introduce new agricultural methods. You have to keep working with everything at your command and eventually certain things will work out. By the time they do, though," he added smiling, "human nature being what it is, a new problem will have popped up. The job never seems to get done, does it?"

"In the long run," Brother said, "motors and people are pretty much the same. I take a motor apart and fix it and it runs for a month or so, and the next thing I know it's back in my shop. I suppose that's why Our Lord gave us the Sacrament of Penance. Excuse me, Father, but speaking of motors, I've left this one too long on its own."

The third night they stayed at Blanca Flor and Brother slept over the motor on the wooden planking.

He awoke around three in the morning, soaked to the skin from a rainstorm. In the morning with a fresh change of clothes, he served all the four masses of the priests, and when the others went ashore for breakfast, he remained aboard working on the motor. It was eleven-thirty in the morning before they got started on the next to last day of their trip.

They reached Ethea at five-thirty that afternoon where Father McGowan and the boy left the launch. There was some discussion on the advisability of going on. If they went on that night to Fortaleza they could make Cavinas the next morning. It was dangerous to travel at night, but in the end they agreed that they ought to risk it.

Bishop Lane took the wheel for a time and then Father Bonner spelled him. At one point he rocked the boat rather dangerously and Brother shouted from the motor pit, "Hey, cut the motor when you do that," and then realizing that he had been rather brusque about it, he added, "Father." Everyone laughed at his consternation.

Father Bonner knew how to handle a boat as well as anyone. What had caused the rocking was his effort to steer and work the spotlight at the same time. Realizing that this could be dangerous, he sent Ignacio the cook up on the roof to man the light.

Bishop Lane and Bishop Danehy both joined Father Bonner in the cabin, partly because it gets lonely up there at night and partly because they were aware of the danger of tree trunks in the river. They wanted to keep a sharp lookout for obstacles, on the theory that several pairs of eyes are better than one.

And they *did* keep a good lookout for sunken tree trunks, but unaware to them, the danger that night lurked not in the river, but above them. A few miles in front of them, a towering jungle tree clung precariously to the river bank; its roots had long since been uncovered and rendered powerless by the current which had cut away the bank and undermined the whole tree. And now as they unknowingly approached the spot where the tree was, it moved slightly in the cool breeze that came off the river, shaking off the last hold it had with the earth, and in God's Divine Providence, hung there balanced for a moment in time, awaiting the destiny for which it had been created.

Brother came up for a few moments. They tried to persuade him to stay awhile, but he was afraid of the motor dying in the darkness. He went back to sit in his favorite spot, on the wooden planking over the motor.

The rest of the missioners were talking in the forward cabin when the tree hit. For the first few dazed moments they thought it had been an explosion. The boat stopped in its tracks, glass shattered in all directions, the lights went out, and the launch appeared to be sinking. Bishop Danehy was the first to recover and shouted for Ignacio. When he got no answer he crawled up on the roof and found him. Father Bonner thought of Brother Gonzaga then.

"Where's Gonzaga?" he asked the Bishop, and then shouted, "Brother, Brother . . . are you all right?" There was no answer. They both ran out of the cabin, heedless of the broken glass and the darkness, toward the motor pit. A huge tree had fallen directly over the motor, missing the forward cabin by a fraction of a second. They heard a moan and found Brother down in the well where the tree had knocked him before it came to rest on the iron railing surrounding the pit. They were able to lift him out. Brother was unconscious, his rosary still in his hand.

Father Bonner gave Brother Gonzaga absolution at once, and then while Bishop Lane remained beside the cot, holding Brother's hand and saying the prayers for the dying, Father Bonner went out to see what could be done about freeing the boat. He remembered that downstream on the other side of the river, they had seen a solitary house.

His "Halloo-o-o-o" shattered the stillness of the jungle. Presently there came a faint answer and finally a canoe with two men. But they had to return for their machetes to cut the tree to free the launch.

Before the men came back, Bishop Lane came out of the cabin. All could tell from his face that Brother had died. "He never regained consciousness," the Bishop said, "and I'm sure he felt no pain. May his soul rest in peace."

By the time the men had hacked the tree free, a launch came along and took them in tow downstream to Ethea. There they laid Brother in the chapel and kept vigil all night with the people from the settlement. The following day Bishop Lane said the Mass and Father Bonner preached. They buried Brother Gonzaga in Ethea, and later moved him to Blanca Flor. Sometime afterwards his remains were taken to Riberalta and buried near those of his old friend, "Tex" Yakota.

As Brother had always wished and prayed, he died on a Feast of the Virgin, the 11th of February.

So in the end, it hadn't really mattered that he had been in an orphanage, or bummed his way across the country, or had been uncertain for awhile about his missionary vocation; or that he had been a Brother instead of a priest. What really mattered was that for the last years of his life he had done "something for God," and had died doing it.

IN RETROSPECT

The preceding chapters have, it is hoped, given enough information about Brother Gonzaga to let the reader know the kind of man he was and the situations in which he found himself while he played the part God had assigned to him. Now the time has come to try to sum him up, to try to say why he was what he was and why he played his part with such unfailing courage and fidelity.

Brother Gonzaga was deeply influenced by two devotions; his devotion to the Little Flower and his devotion to the Blessed Mother marked him very early, as early as we can form any idea of his spiritual life. To use Father Stern's description of him, devotion to the Little Flower and especially to our Blessed Mother "just beamed and oozed out of him"; and this was the case a couple of years before he came to Maryknoll.

And yet perhaps "devotion" is not the right word to describe his relation to the Mother of Jesus and to the saint of Lisieux. His attitude was both more and less than what we ordinarily mean by devotion. These two were more to him than the object of a devotion; they were his prophets, his instructors, his guides. And the lesson that he learned from them was to go, not to them, but to the Head, to Jesus in the Blessed Sacrament, to God in all this wonderful world, and to God in men.

His whole spiritual life showed the influence of the Little Flower's person and doctrine, of the lesson that she was and the lessons that she taught. He himself tells us that it was to the reading of her autobiography that he owed his vocation to the missionary life. When, not long after he joined Maryknoll, he felt that he was called to be a Trappist, he stated that, as a Trappist, he would consider himself "a cloistered Maryknoller." There can be no doubt that he was imitating her when he went to Gethsemani, and that he was convinced that God was calling him there. When he found that the cloistered life was not for him, he was puzzled and could not quite believe it for years.

The Little Flower is one of those rare saints to whom it was given to introduce not so much a new spiritual fashion—much less a mere spiritual fad—as a new style or form of the spiritual life, if we may use the term as it is used when we speak of a new style of painting or a new architectural form. Perhaps after all it is better to use her own term—a biblical one—and say that she introduced a new spiritual way. The characteristic marks of her spirituality are very well known. She had, for instance, a strikingly clear and vivid realization of the insignificance of time. "It is a mistake," according to her, "to give the name of life to something that has to end . . . Jesus thinks nothing of time, since He is eternal." Along with this, she had an overwhelming desire for eternity, but not for an eternity of rest and repose. "I would never rest until the end of the world," she says, "as long as there are souls to save; but when the Angel says, 'Time is no more,' then I will rest and enjoy myself." All her life she dedicated herself to the saving of souls, and she knew the secret of it: "Jesus pays attention only to love." She knew that she would be satisfied at the moment of her death if she could have but one soul to offer to Jesus.

Perhaps the most distinctive mark of her approach to God and to souls was her very strong conviction that she could work for the members of Christ best, as she herself put it, by going to the Head. And when she went to the Head, to Jesus, she did so in her own original way; generally she did not work for individual souls directly but for the souls of priests. She knew that if she could succeed in making priests what they ought to be, the people would be what Jesus wanted them to be. So she went directly to Jesus in her striving to be of help to priests and to the people for whom the priests were responsible to the Head.

This is, in brief, the way that Brother Gonzaga was trying to follow even when he came to Maryknoll in order, as he phrased it, to do "something grand for God." Despite the many and great external differences between his life and the life of the saint in the cloister at Lisieux, the inner spirit was the same. His lot was not cast in the garden of Gethsemani, but on the roads of Ohio and the rivers of Bolivia; and yet everywhere he was trying to do the same work and in the same fashion.

The conditions of his early life do not bear a close

resemblance to those of Thérèse Martin. It is true, of course, that Brother lost his father about the same age as Thérèse lost her mother, but the consequences were very different. Thérèse, when she lost her mother, did not lose the wonderful home that had always been hers; but for Brother the loss of his father had meant life in institutions from a very early age. He is a proof that these institutions did their work well, but the misfortune of losing a father and being separated from the rest of the family, like his later experience of the depression and the difficulties of finding work and even enough to eat, left its mark on him. His own life helped to form in him a deep understanding of and an instinctive sympathy for the weak, and down-trodden, the misfits of this world. When he spoke of the poor, it was with a personal interest. He could not under any circumstances refuse anything to anybody. Others thought that people imposed on his sympathy. Those who borrowed money from him were not good risks. Those who borrowed his tools were likely to misuse them or forget to return them. He went off annually on vacation charged with various commissions for priests and people. He came back loaded down with things that he had bought for other people, sometimes because they had requested him to buy them, sometimes because he could not bear not to have things to give away.

There was nothing he would not do to help others. It did not matter to him that the people he was trying to help were often untrustworthy, unreliable, ungrateful. He could never bring himself to believe that his generosity to people could hurt them. And who can say —who indeed would wish to say—that he was wrong? If one of us had helped them with his recklessness (and without his trust in them or his love for them), our generosity might well have done them more harm than good; but his trust in them and his love for them helped to make them better people than they normally were. He inoculated them, so to speak, against themselves, and for the moment, and sometimes for much more than the moment, helped to lift them above themselves and enable them to act in accordance with his confidence in them. Perhaps the most amazing thing about him was the fact that people often enough did not disappoint him. They did at times repay the money and return the tools unharmed. And they always repaid the interest he took in them by doing him a good turn when they had the opportunity, and assisting him when they were able to do so.

Early misfortune, separation from the family, poverty, the hard struggle for existence did not warp him or make him grasping and self-centered. Deliberately, with the grace of God, he had always managed to see the stars. And all his life people seem to have helped him and wanted to help him. His letters are filled with the idea of gratitude and fidelity, of showing that he was grateful by being faithful. Instead of feeling sorry for himself that he had lost something irreplaceable when he was deprived of father and home, he chose to be grateful for the devoted care that the Sisters and the Brothers had lavished on him. He seems to have had a special gift for remembering the good things that had happened to him and for forgetting the hard things.

There is not in his letters a single instance of anything one could call self-pity. Yet he frequently enough mentions the hard conditions under which he lived and worked, and in his conversations he did not make any effort to pretend that they were not hard. The heat, for example, bothered him greatly and often made sleep difficult or impossible; but at such times he used to remind himself of Cochabamba and his vacations there, the good high air that God had given him to breathe and the mountains that He had given him to see. Brother was quite aware that unreasonable demands were made on him at times, and that now and then he was forced to put in long hours of work at jobs which he could have been spared if others had been a little more thoughtful or a little less careless. When incidents like this occurred he was likely to bristle. A number of people observed that his first reaction in such circumstances was to flare up. The surprising thing is that he did not flare up. He was able to control the instinct to lash out at the offender and to tell him off, or at least to keep himself from speaking in the heat of the first angry wave of emotion. No one seems to recall any incident where his control failed, but many recall incidents where they were astounded that it did not fail. To a very few he did confide his awareness that others imposed upon him, but it was without bitterness or resentment. There is no doubt that he was asked to do more than one man could reasonably have been expected to do, but this is what always happens to the man who is ready to render a service and seems anxious under any circumstance to do so.

It is not likely that Brother spent much time nursing grievances. Here again the Little Flower was probably his greatest support. She wanted to do her work for souls, for the world, by working through priests; and she wanted to work through priests by working for them, by going to Jesus to intercede for them. Brother was always talking about the people, about their salvation. He was thinking, as his words often showed, of their salvation as coming to them through the Church, and in the Pando, through the ministers of the Church, the Maryknoll priests there.

He was bound by many ties to the priests who were in the Pando when he arrived. His relations with them went back to their student days either at Maryknoll or Clarks Summit. He fitted at once into the community of the priests in the Beni, and was never a stranger or an outsider when he was with priests. A number of the priests in the Pando were good athletes and Brother was well aware of the prestige their athletic prowess brought to the Church. He was proud of them when they went out on the basketball court and won a game from one of the town teams. He sometimes was on the priests' team himself, and he played basketball with the same intensity with which he did everything. He played to win. In this case, victory meant more than a victory for the team. It meant a victory for the Church too. The people came to look on the priests a little differently when they saw them on the basketball court. A victory for the priests meant added respect for them and for the Church. To be accepted as a basketball player might lead to being accepted eventually as a teacher and a priest.

Brother, however, did not merely work alongside the priests as helper, by keeping their machines in order, or by playing basketball on their team, or by taking a hand in a card game in the evening, although he did all these things, enjoyed doing them and was aware of their importance. Like the Little Flower, he made a habit of going to the Head, especially to Jesus in the Blessed Sacrament. From the time he came to Maryknoll it was noticed that he seemed to love to be in the chapel; and wherever he was stationed, if you wanted him in a hurry in the hours when he was ordinarily not at work, your best bet was to try the chapel or the church first. During these precious hours of prayer, especially in the evening, he was undoubtedly praying to the Head for the members, praying for the priests of the Pando whose responsibility it was to look after the members of Christ in the Pando. Every one of the priests appreciated his prayers even more than his work, and they considered his work invaluable.

What Brother did not know—what he never even suspected—was that in his life, in his very person, he himself was an inspiration for the priests, reminding them day in and day out of the things that really mattered. Missionary priests are always at work in surroundings which constitute a threat to their priestly ideals. The Faith is unknown in some parts of the mission world; in others, as in northern Bolivia, although it is known to everyone, it is known only in the most sketchy and superficial way. The religious ignorance of the people is very great. The missionary is always working, if not in a black-out, at least in a dim-out. He is in constant danger of letting the light that is in him be overcome by the ever-threatening darkness. The priest sees so many people who refuse to take God seriously that he may easily find himself taking God less and less seriously. Some one has said that the greatest danger to a priest in an almost completely pagan mission is the danger of being converted to paganism. In the Pando the danger is not so serious; but there is a danger of succumbing gradually to the widespread indifference. When there is a man like Brother Gonzaga around, it is not so easy to succumb.

He had very high ideal for priests and Sisters and Brothers. He did not often speak directly about this. But you knew that it was there. The black eyes which burned in him with such intensity revealed the intensity of his spiritual life. He never did his good works that they might shine before men; but he did them and they shone. And there is no priest who was in the Pando with him who does not still praise his Father in heaven for the encouragement it was to know Brother and to observe his life. At meals in Riberalta, when he was home off the rivers, or during the recreation periods which he sometimes managed to fit into his crowded day, he was one of the group; but the level of the group was raised by his presence, and everyone felt that it was. If, however, anyone had told him how much he did for the priests of the Pando and, through them, for the Church in the Pando, simply by being what he was, he would have had a great laugh.

Father August Kircher remembers seeing Brother reading the magazine *The Priest* during his vacation in Cochabamba. Father Kircher spoke to him about this, and learned that it was a favorite of his. It is likely that Brother also read other clerical magazines fairly regularly. He was quite at home with priests when they were talking shop, whether it was about canonical or pastoral or theological matters. It is probable that he read up on subjects in which he either knew the priests were interested or hoped they would be interested. He was never ill at ease or bored when such matters were discussed, and he could take an intelligent part in discussions where normally a layman would be at sea. Had he been suddenly changed to some place where he would not have been mixing regularly and familiarly with priests, he would probably have been very much at a loss for some time. There can be no doubt that he had a great influence for good on all the priests in the Pando and on the other priests whom he met during his annual vacations.

Some of these characteristics he had acquired by imitating the Little Flower or under her guidance; for others he was indebted to the Blessed Mother. It is not important to define the exact amount of influence each of these had in making him the wonderful Brother that he was to priests and people. But the most characteristic quality of his spiritual life was simplicity, if we take the word in its Gospel meaning, and for this he was surely indebted to both our Lady and to St. Thérèse.

The simple man is the man who is clean of heart; his simplicity is the opposite of the duplicity which the

Gospels frequently call hypocrisy. Hypocrisy is the characteristic vice of the superficially religious person, of the man who is outwardly faithful to his religious duties but carries them out primarily with an eye to his own comfort and reputation and well-being in this world. A hypocrite is not pure of heart, and he does not see God. We speak of a clean cut, when we mean a cut that has no jagged edges and no complications; of a clean sweep, when the sweep we are referring to is complete; of a clean hit, when the batter has really earned his way to first base and there is nothing phony about the way he reached it. A clean heart includes all of these things, and something more, because the heart here stands for what is most human in man, the source from which proceed his thoughts, his words, his resolutions.

The man who is clean of heart sees that if it is reasonable to give God any place at all in our lives, it makes no sense to give Him anything but the *first* place. Such a man dedicates himself utterly to God and is ready for anything that God may send him. He sees that he may never succeed in loving God with his *whole* heart and his *whole* soul and his *whole* mind and *all* his strength in this world, but he knows that to attempt anything less is to insult God. When the man who is clean of heart prays, He does not do so in order to impress the people who may see him at prayer. When he gives alms, he does not let his left hand know what his right hand is doing. Not only does he shrink from showing off his piety before others; he is afraid even to let himself think of himself in this connection.

Someone has said that purity of heart consists in willing one thing. And no one can will one thing, unless that thing is itself perfect and infinite, that is, unless it is God. This is the secret of the clean of heart, the source of their intensity and their unity, of their integrity and completeness. When you came in contact with Brother Gonzaga, you felt that you were enjoying an unusual experience. The spiritual atmosphere seemed more highly charged. You felt that here was a man who saw God more clearly than the rest of us who have not really made up our minds that no sensible person can ask for more than God. Here was a man who did not seem interested in ensuring that he had the support and the admiration of other men; and yet he attracted men, as only those attract them who look for God alone.

The impression of intensity and eagerness which you experienced when you spoke with Brother was simply another aspect of his evangelical simplicity, its inevitable, its necessary, consequence. Even a first meeting with him made you aware that there were spiritual depths in him corresponding to the black depths of his striking eyes. He became a Maryknoll Brother in order to dedicate his life to the service of God, to do what he thought God was demanding of him. He never bothered much about what was the best thing for Charlie Chilutti. Whether or not Charlie would be satisfied and happy did not seem to him important. He was never much concerned about methods of cultivating the spiritual life. He did not have to be, because his daily work was accomplished without losing sight of God, and his times of prayer were simply opportunities to pay more attention to God. He could indulge in small talk without letting others see that he thought it a waste of time but, as one priest remarked, he never did so when he was with anyone alone. Then, somehow, without ostentation, without one's realizing what was happening, the conversation quickly turned to religious themes, and one found oneself talking about the Little Flower and her little way, or about the work of the missions or about the people, especially about the people who did not take too readily to religious things, the people who were hard to bring back to the sacraments; for all of these Brother Gonzaga had sympathy and charity enough to cover all the multitude of their sins and many more besides. It is only when one (at least) of the two parties to a dialogue is pure in heart that such a conversation can succeed in being natural. Anyone could see that any other conversation would have been highly unnatural to him. When you were talking alone with him, it would seem to you as unfitting to discuss the baseball scores as it would if you were talking to the Blessed Mother herself. "Out of the abundance of the heart, the mouth speaks."

The present writer, when he was in Bolivia in 1948 to give a series of retreats, made a note at the time of the first retreat he preached. It took place at Cochabamba, and the note is dated Sept. 29, 1948. It reads: "Brother Gonzaga made it (the retreat at Cochabamba). Lovely a character as ever. Told me with great enthusiasm of the work the priests were doing, their zeal, etc. Probably understands the problems of the Pando as well as anyone. What is more, he sees visions and dreams of what it might be and may yet be—from a spiritual point of view mainly." This stenographic report made at the time gives fairly accurately the impression that Brother made, not only on the writer, but on all.

He was a man who went the whole way, without counting the cost and without dragging his feet. He had his experience of sorrow and joy here in this world. May we not hope that he is now experiencing the Glorious Mysteries and helping the Little Flower in that apostolate of hers which is to continue until the last trumpet sounds? "Blessed are the clean of heart, for they shall see God."

J.F.M.